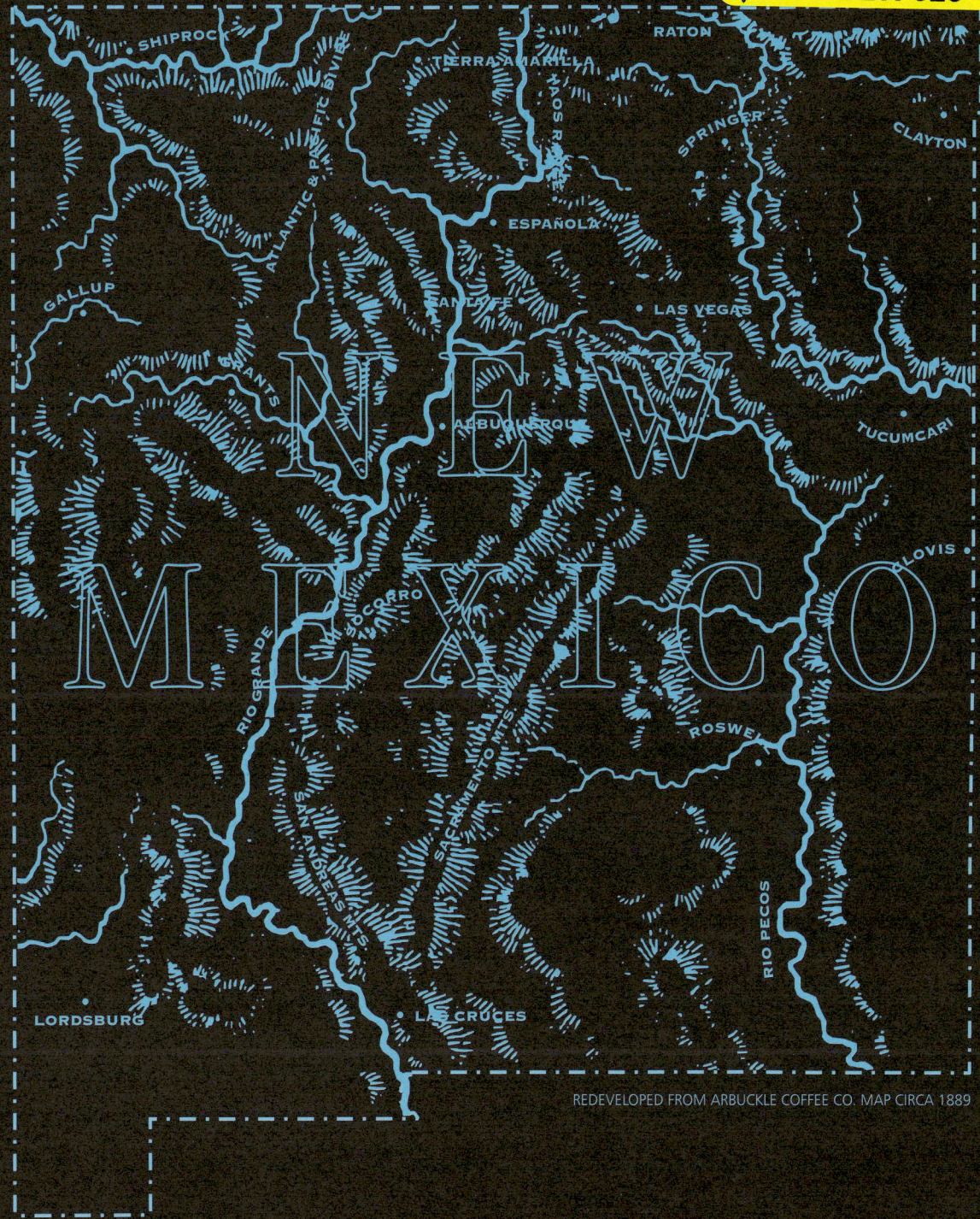

Y0-DBX-528

NEW MEXICO

SHIPROCK
RATON
TERRA AMARILLA
TAOS R.
CLAYTON
SPRINGER
ATLANTIC & PACIFIC R.R.
ESPAÑOLA
GALLUP
SANTA FE
LAS VEGAS
GRANTS
ALBUQUERQUE
TUCUMCARI
SOCORRO
RIO GRANDE
CLOVIS
SACRAMENTO MTS.
ROSWELL
SAN ANDREAS MTS.
RIO PECOS
LORDSBURG
LAS CRUCES

REDEVELOPED FROM ARBUCKLE COFFEE CO. MAP CIRCA 1889

From Tony

Early Signs of Enchantment

New Mexico Roadside Nostalgia

To Inez —
Enjoy this journey
through ol' New Mexico
Best Wishes —

Andy Marquez

12/2004

Andy Marquez

Acknowledgements

Acknowledgements

I would like to thank a few people who were instrumental in helping me to produce this second book in the aging sign series. Todd Anderson, for his clean, sharp and easy to follow design work. Ethan Jantzer and Kelly Sylvester of Reed Photo for their assistance in converting a creative photograph into a visually appealing print. My life-time friend, Chuck Williams, for his insistence that I buy a GPS unit for my work, and his assistance in helping me mark all the waypoints of the signs. Ruth Gore, of the Rio Grande Arts and Crafts Festival in Albuquerque, for encouraging me to do a New Mexico version of roadside nostalgia. Kathy Redmond, and Pacifica for their excellent printing of these books.

My wife, Teresa, and children, Chris, Leanne and Nikki, for their continued understanding that quite often Dad has to take off out of town to pursue these creative endeavors. And finally, to my mother, Gloria, who has always been there, giving to us, generously, her grace and her wisdom.

Copyright © 2004 by Castle Q Publishing
All rights reserved
First Edition
Manufacturing by Pacifica Communications
Book design by Todd Anderson of Desktop Studio
ISBN 0-9743291-8-5
1. Photography

Castle Q Publishing
2509 West Main Street
Littleton, Colorado 80120
303.797.6040
www.andymarquez.com

All photos shown in this book are available as limited edition fine art prints.

The surging popularity of "Last Signs of the Frontier" sparked my desires to do a second book of aging signs. Deciding where to do it was easy. New Mexico is not only my neighboring state, but a favorite of mine… *The Land of Enchantment.* I have traveled the state often, showing my art and photographing in Albuquerque, Santa Fe, and Taos.

I planned a two day trip to New Mexico in the spring of 2003, crossing the border from Trinidad, Colorado into Raton, New Mexico. East to Clayton, south to Tucumcari, west to Gallup, north to Farmington, I was somewhat disappointed in the numbers of signs I found, far fewer than what I would need to make this book a reality. But I kept my hope to the highway, as I closed in on my first 1,000 miles and at last found my treasure of signs in Tierra Amarilla. It took me nearly a year of shooting to complete the photography for the book. I would spend the night at a hotel and by sunrise be back on the road hunting for signs until there was no light left in the day. I would stop only momentarily to shoot a sign that has survived the test of time.

Driving down Route 66, gave me a greater appreciation for what cross country travel was like when the world was not so fast paced. Today, though most of the images in this book still can be seen, some have vanished and others will follow shortly.

Discover the past as you ride along the pages of New Mexico's highways, and remember that each of these signs represented the hopes and dreams of an individual, a family, a society.

Enjoy,

Andy Marquez

Andy Marquez

Introduction

Table of Contents

The North Side of I-40

N36° 42.1
W106° 33.0

Tierra Amarilla, near downtown

Seboyeta, Hwy 279

N35° 10.5
W107° 23.3

El Rito, Hwy 554

Española, downtown

N35° 59.4
W106° 04.7

Raton, Hwy 87

Clayton, Hwy 64/87

N36° 27.7
W103° 11.1

Dulce, Hwy 64

Des Moines, Hwy 64/87

N35° 45.7
W103° 50.1

MAXWELL HOUSE

Robert

GROCERY

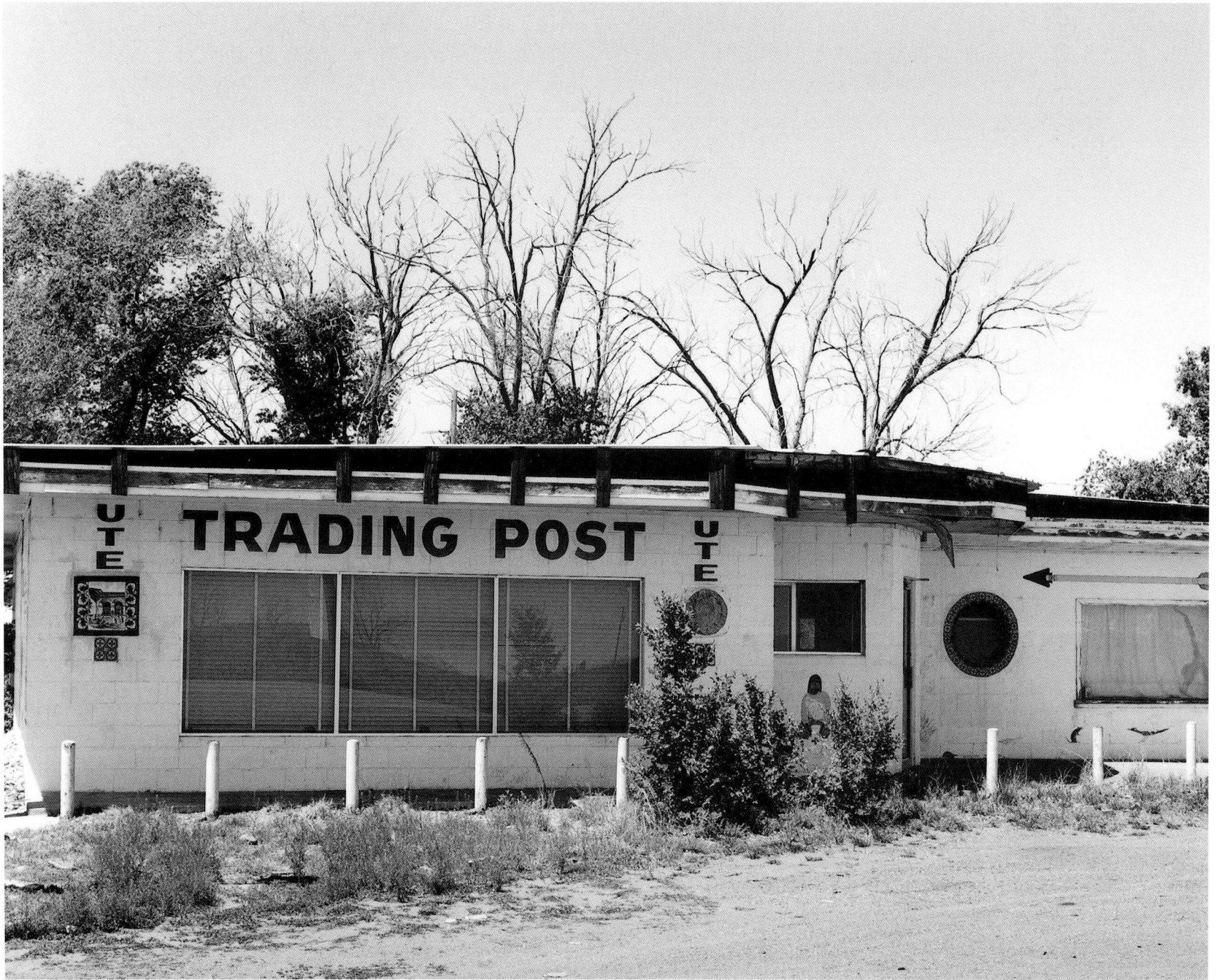

Logan, Hwy 54

N35° 22.2
W103° 24.7

N36° 42.1
W106° 33.5

Tierra Amarilla, Hwy 84

Española, Hwy 84

N36° 12.5
W105° 57.1

Embudo, Hwy 68

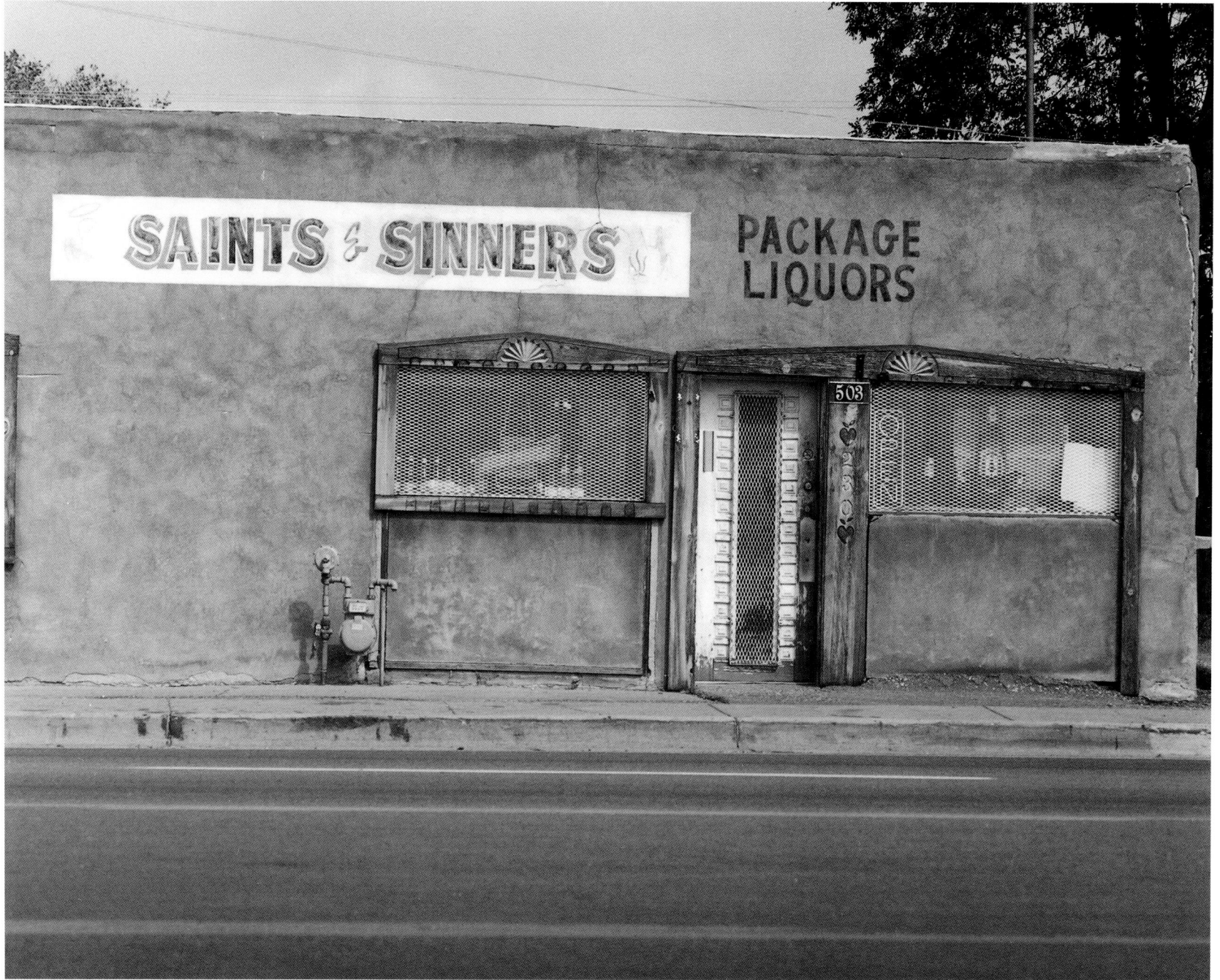

Española, Hwy 285

N35° 59.3
W106° 03.8

Lumberton, Hwy 64

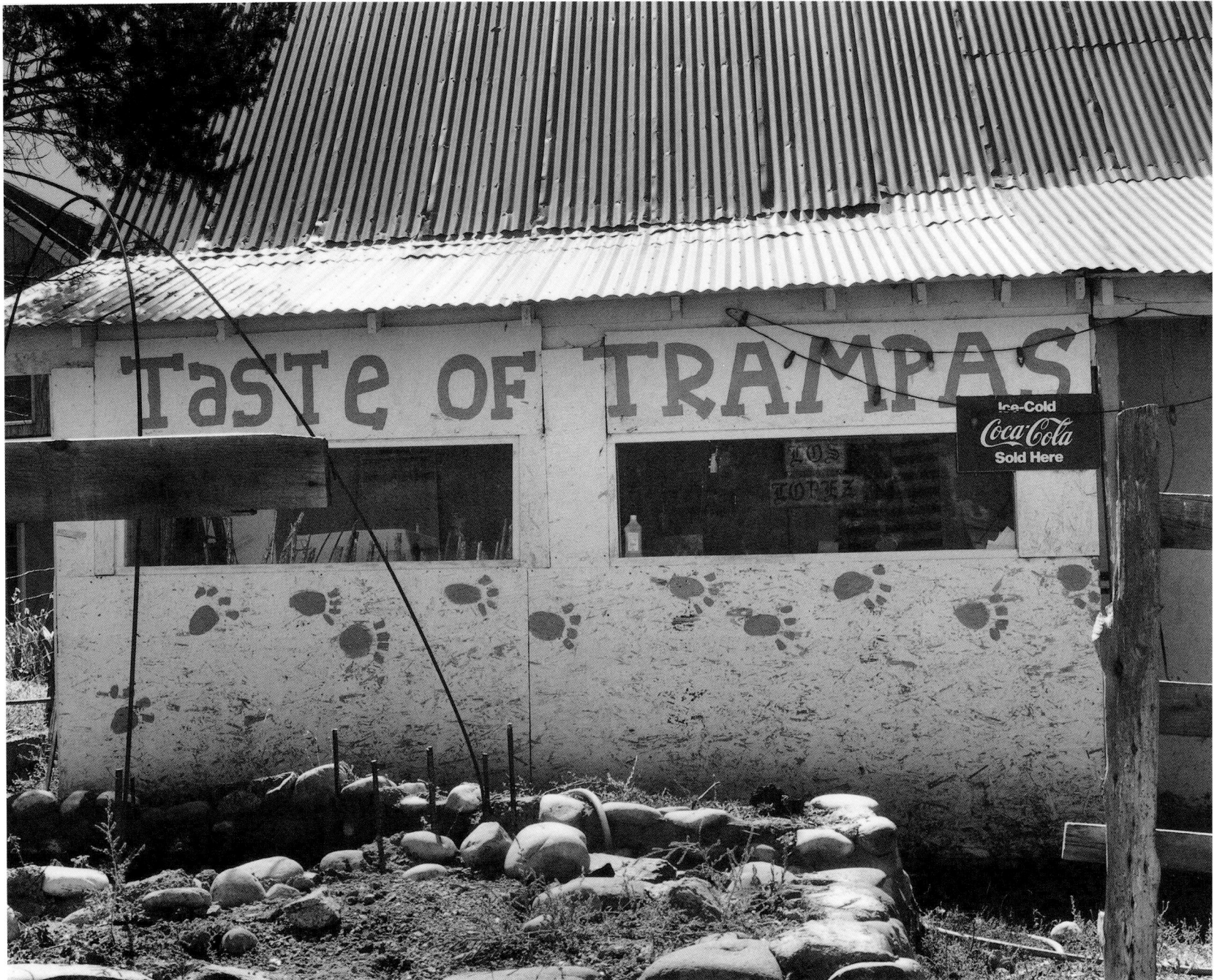

22

Las Trampas, Hwy 76

N36° 07.9
W105° 45.6

BROKEN ARROW

MOTEL

N36° 21.7
W104° 35.7

Springer, off I-25

24

Raton, downtown

N36° 54.0
W107° 26.3

COON-HOLLER CAFE

N36° 05.3
W106° 58.5

La Jara, Hwy 96

Laguna Pueblo, off I-40

N35° 02.2
W107° 23.0

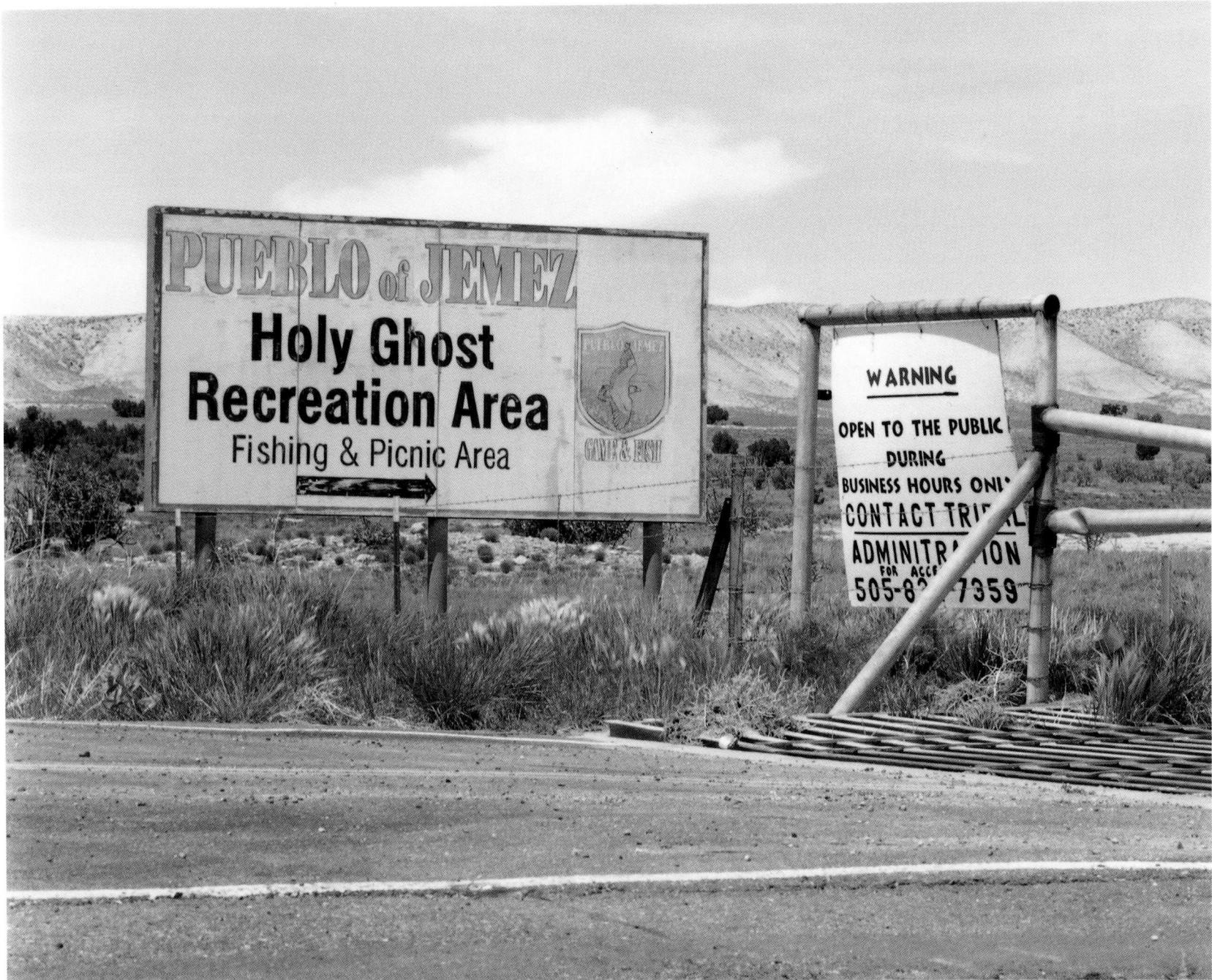

N35° 43.4
W106° 56.4

Jemez Pueblo, Hwy 44

Tucumcari, downtown

N35° 10.8
W103° 43.6

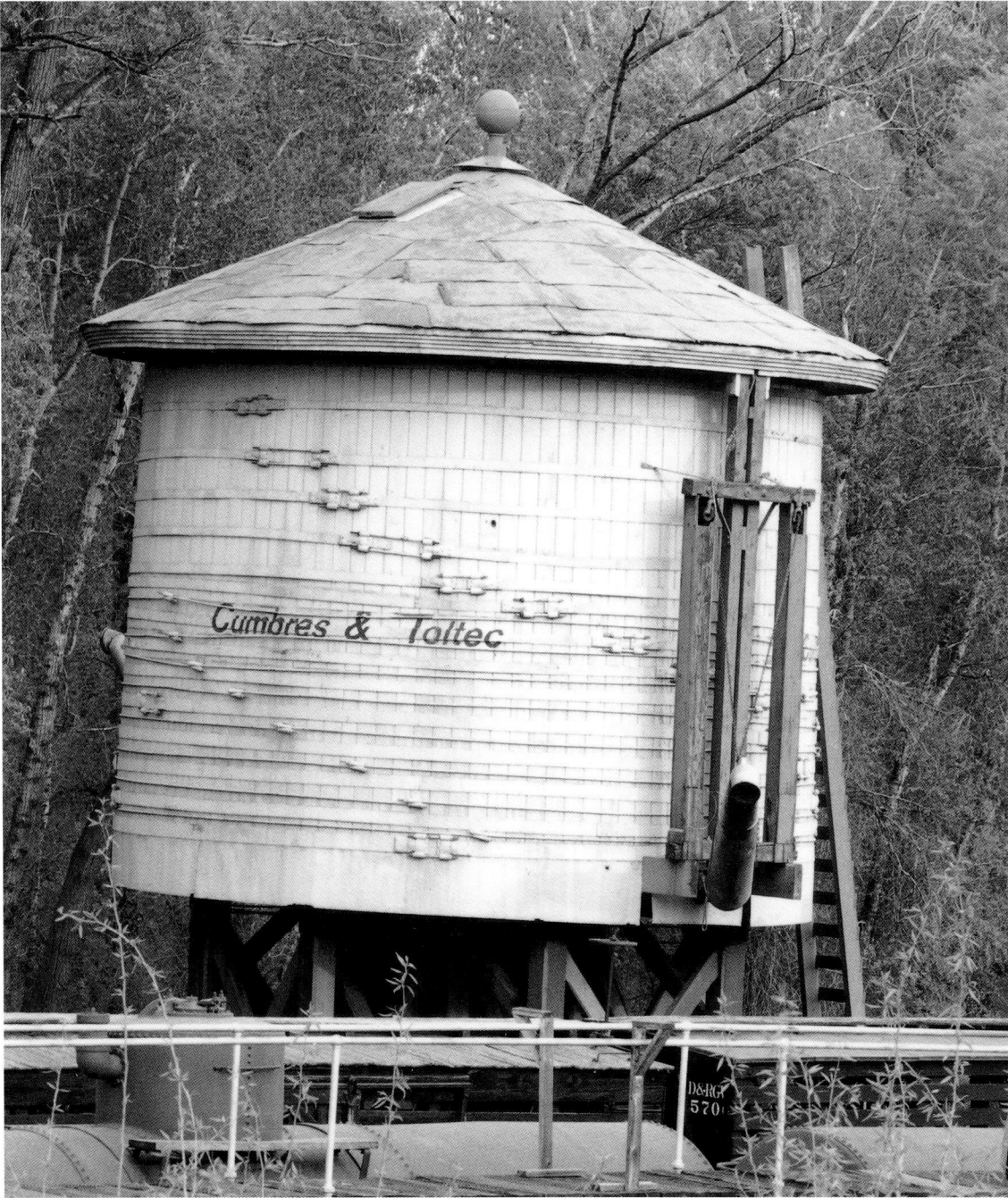

N36° 54.2
W106° 34.7

Chama, Hwy 17

Española, downtown

N35° 59.4
W106° 04.7

N36° 00.4
W104° 42.8

Wagon Mound, off I-25

Ojo Caliente, Hwy 285

N36° 18.2
W106° 02.7

Nara Visa, Hwy 54

Tierra Amarilla, downtown

N36° 42.0
W106° 33.1

Las Vegas, off the Plaza

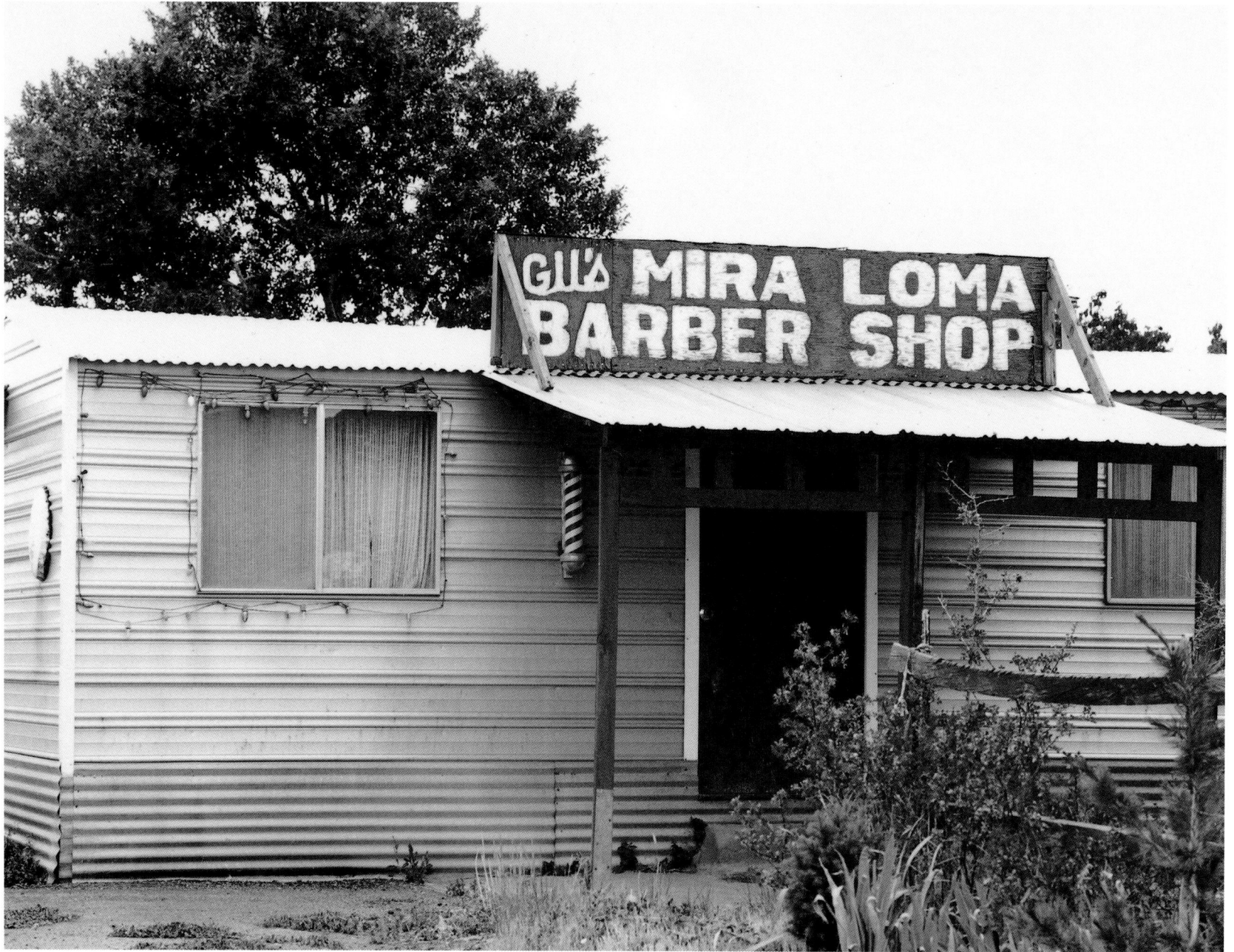

Tierra Amarilla, Hwy 84

N36° 42.1
W106° 33.5

N36° 42.1
W106° 33.5

Tierra Amarilla, Hwy 84

U.S. POST OFFICE
WAGON MOUND. N.MEX 87752

Wagon Mound, off I-25

N36° 00.4
W104° 42.8

NAVAJO TEXTILES INC.

N35° 35.6
W105° 13.5

Las Vegas, The Plaza

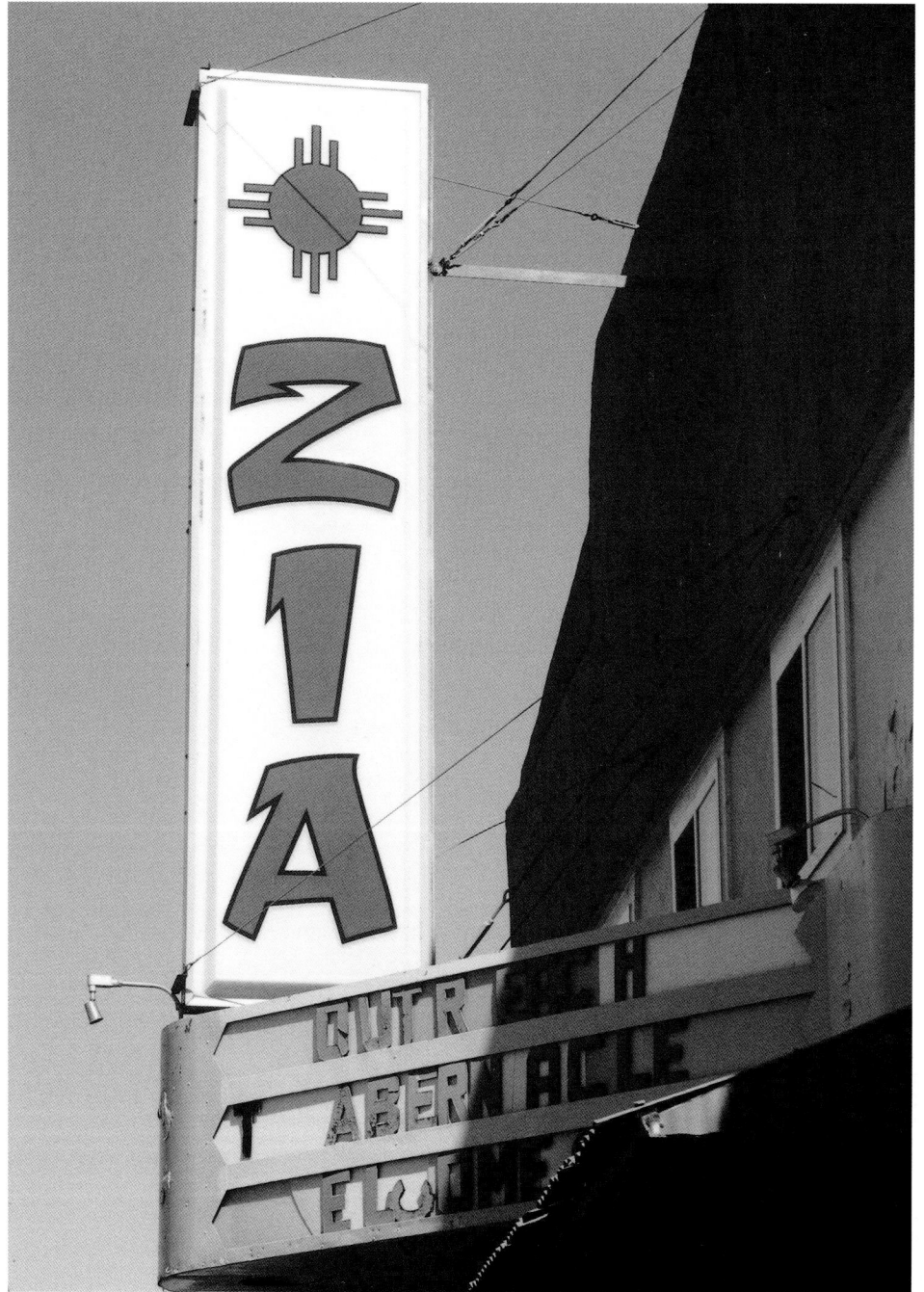

Springer, downtown

N36° 21.7
W104° 35.7

N36° 42.0
W106° 33.1

Tierra Amarilla, downtown

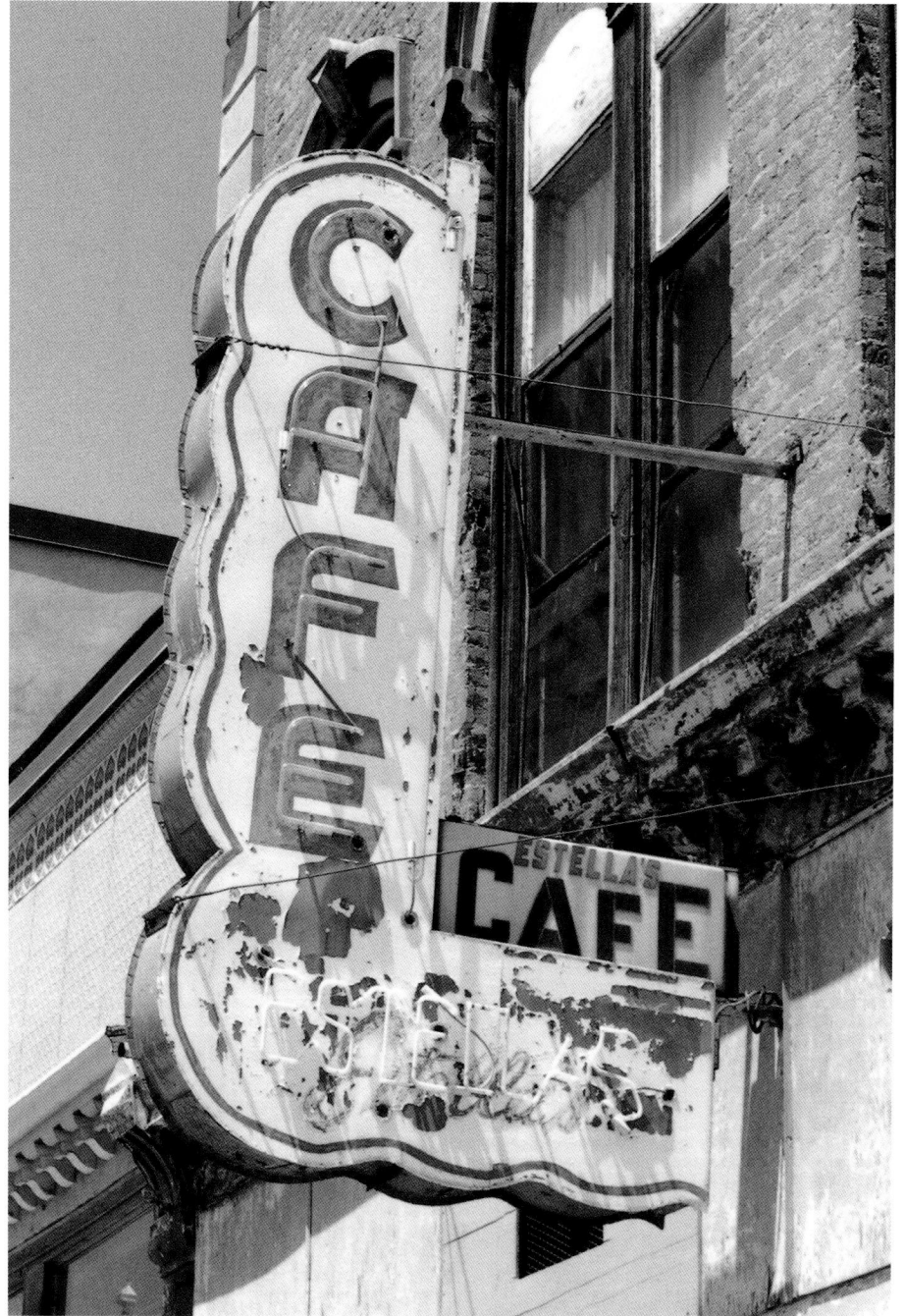

Las Vegas, off the Plaza

N35° 35.6
W105° 13.6

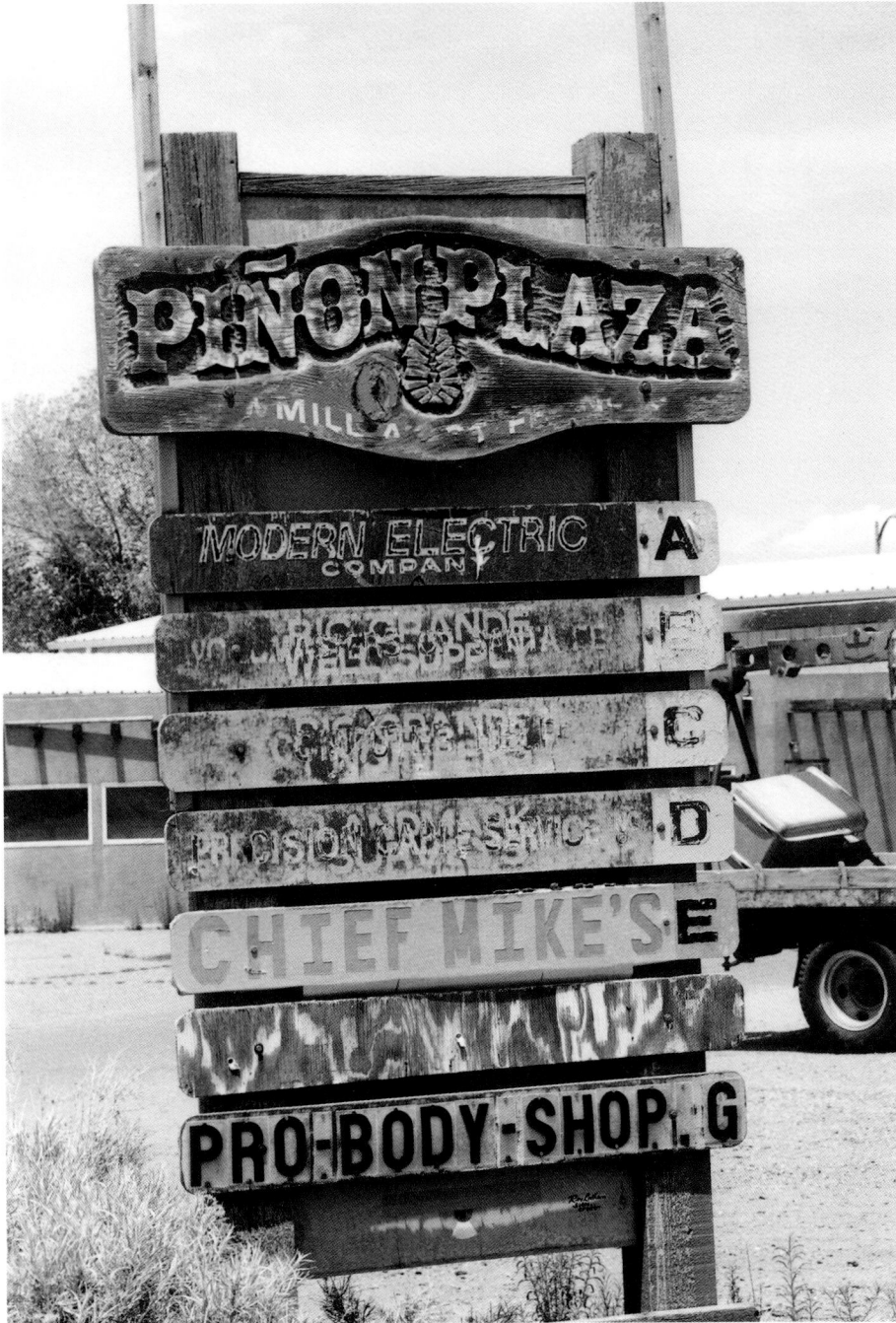

PIÑON PLAZA
A MILL

MODERN ELECTRIC COMPANY A
RIO GRANDE WELL SUPPLY B
C
PRECISION CABLE SERVICE D
CHIEF MIKE'S E
PRO-BODY-SHOP G

N35° 38.5
W105° 57.5

Santa Fe, Sawmill Rd.

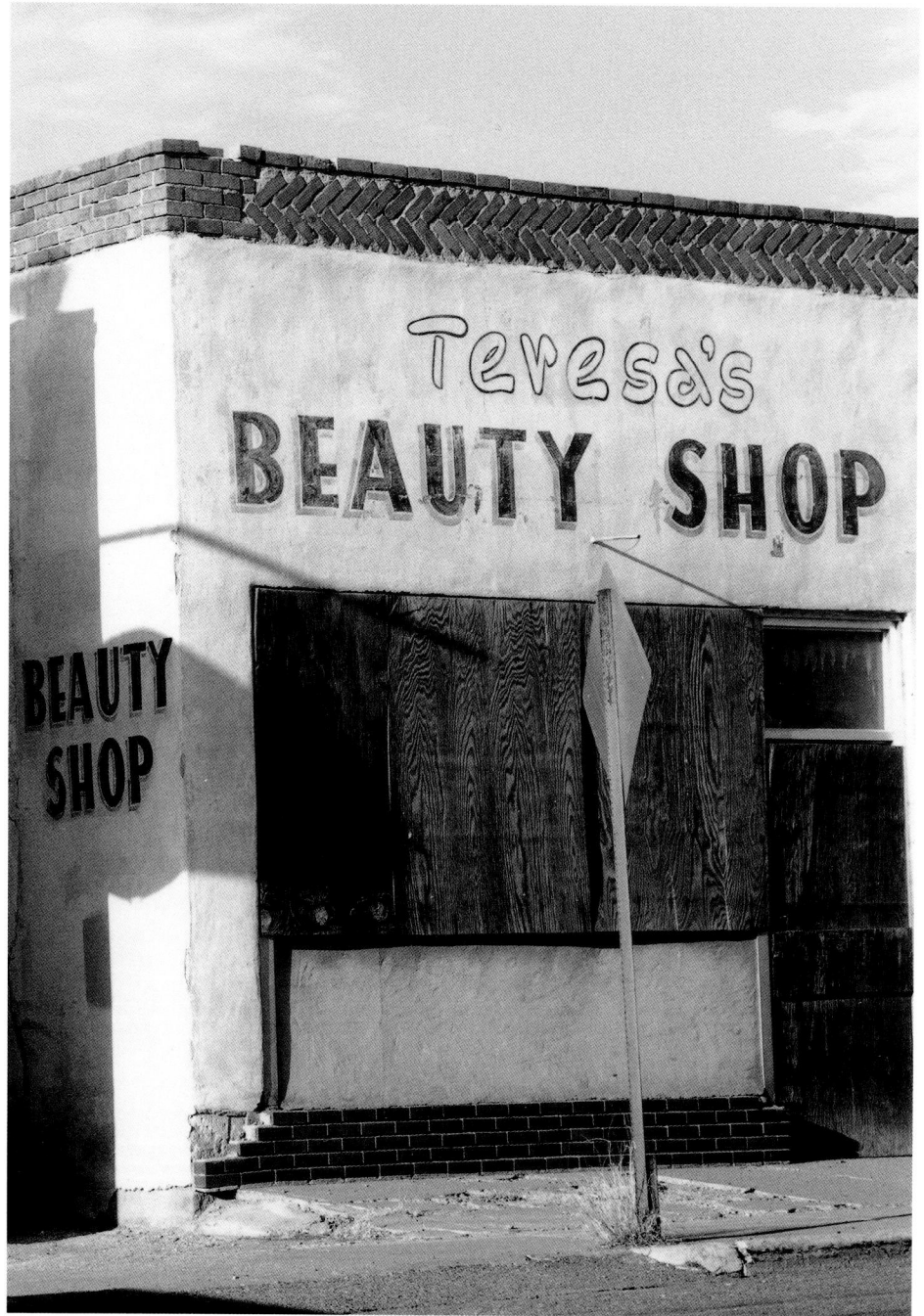

Española, downtown

N35° 59.4
W106° 04.7

Rinconada, Hwy 68

Tres Piedras, Hwy 285

N36° 38.7
W105° 58.1

N36° 10.9
W106° 57.5

Regina, Hwy 96

Des Moines, Hwy 64/87

N36° 45.7
W103° 50.1

N36° 03.5
W105° 48.6

Truchas, Hwy 76

La Jara, Hwy 96

N36° 05.3
W106° 58.5

N36° 42.0
W106° 33.1

Tierra Amarilla, downtown

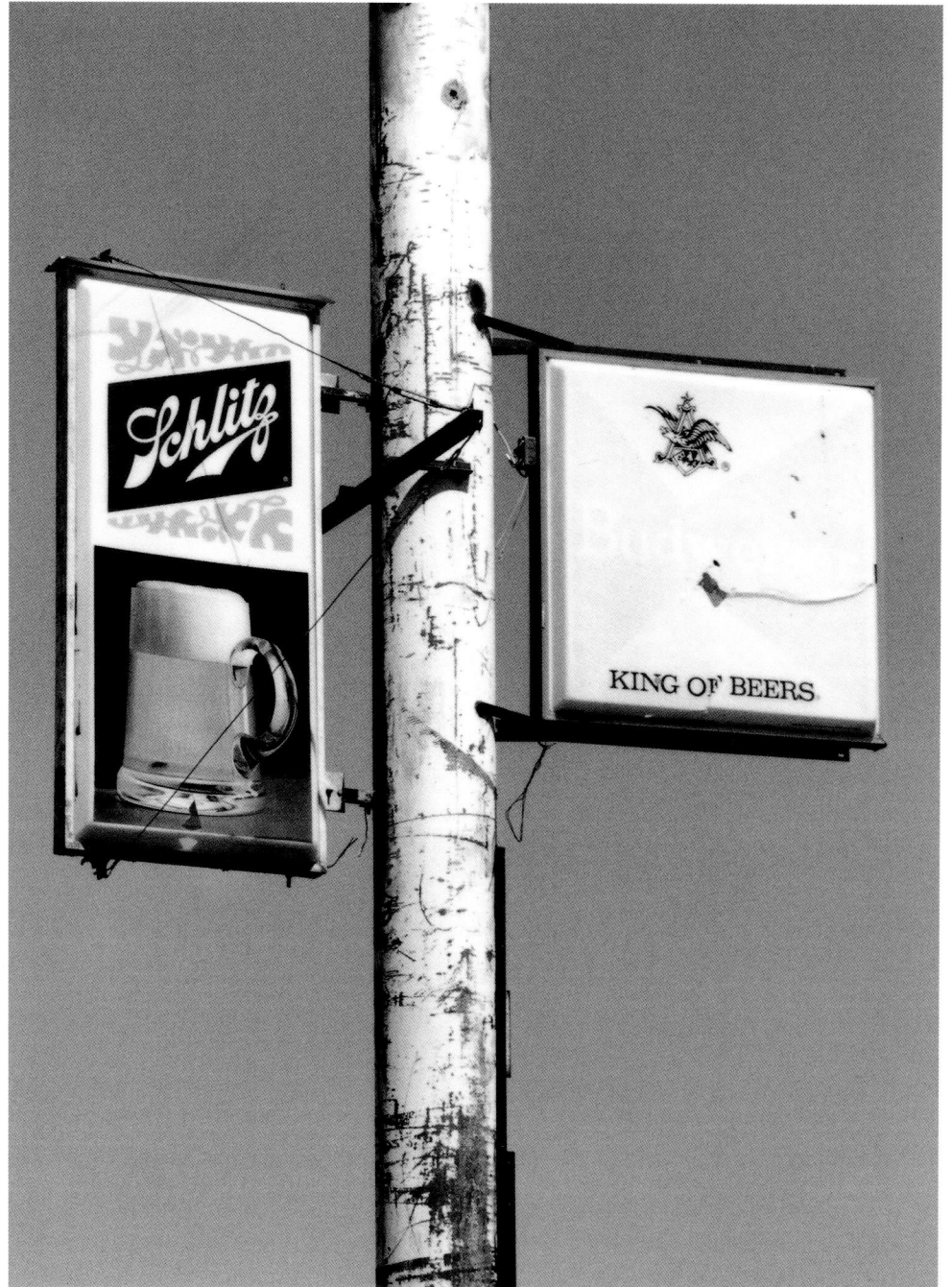

Endee Exit, I-40

N35° 10.5
W103° 06.3

Nara Visa, Hwy 54

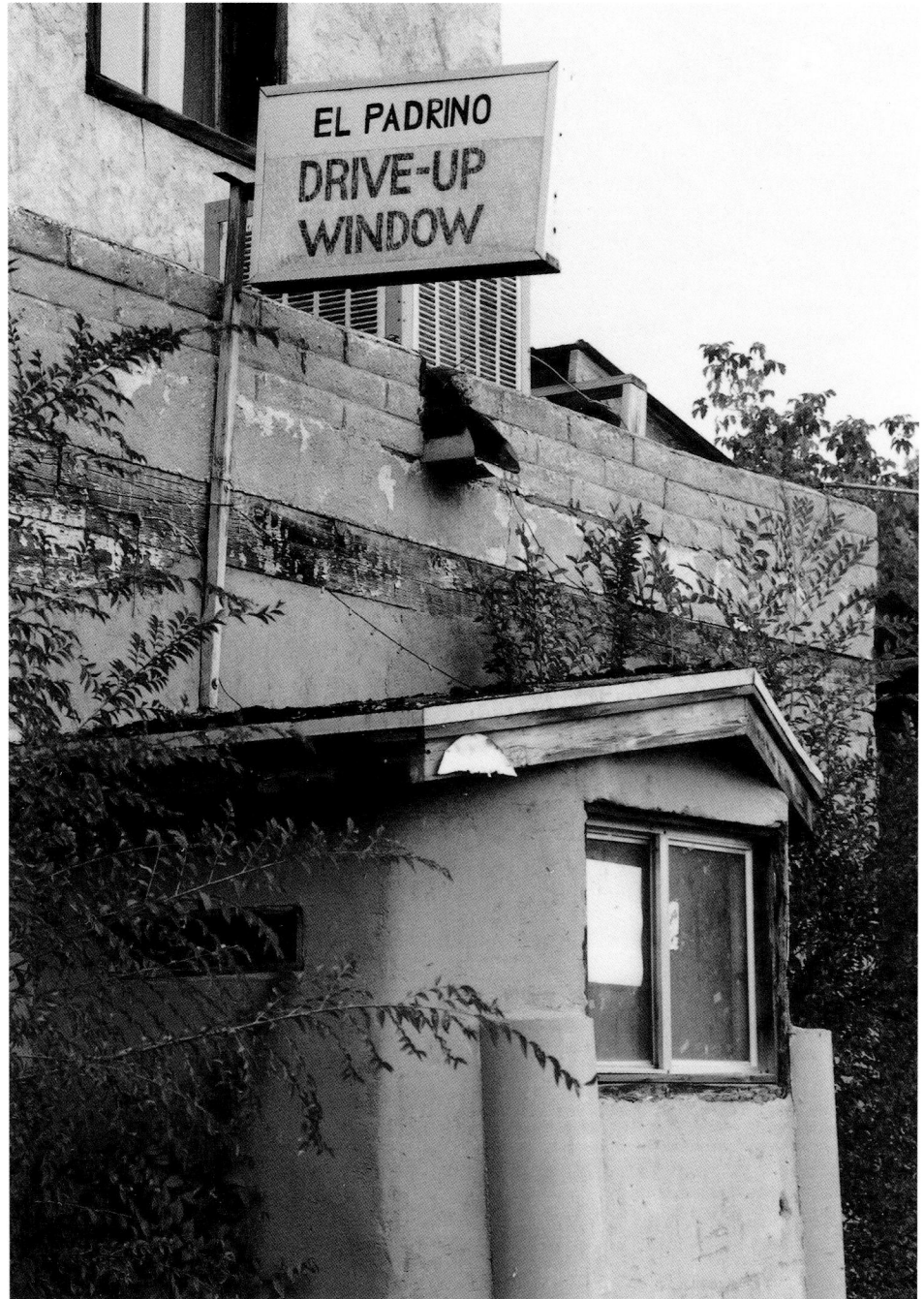

Rancho de Taos, Hwy 68

N36° 21.7
W105° 36.3

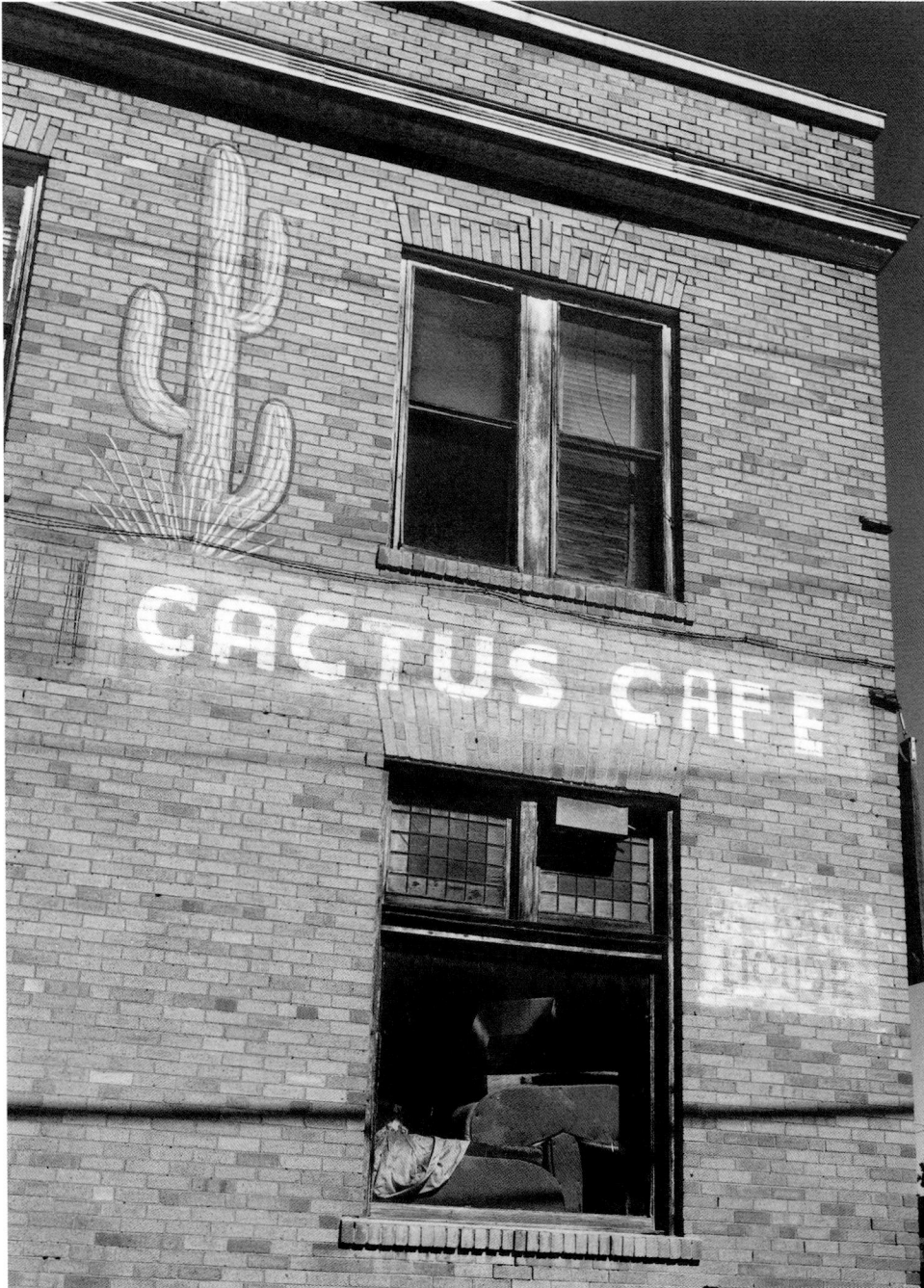

N36° 21.7
W104° 35.7

Springer, downtown

Espanola, Hwy 68

N36° 05.5
W106° 02.9

N36° 47.1
W108° 41.0

Shiprock, Hwy 64

Historic Old Route 66

N35° 06.4
W103° 19.9

San Jon

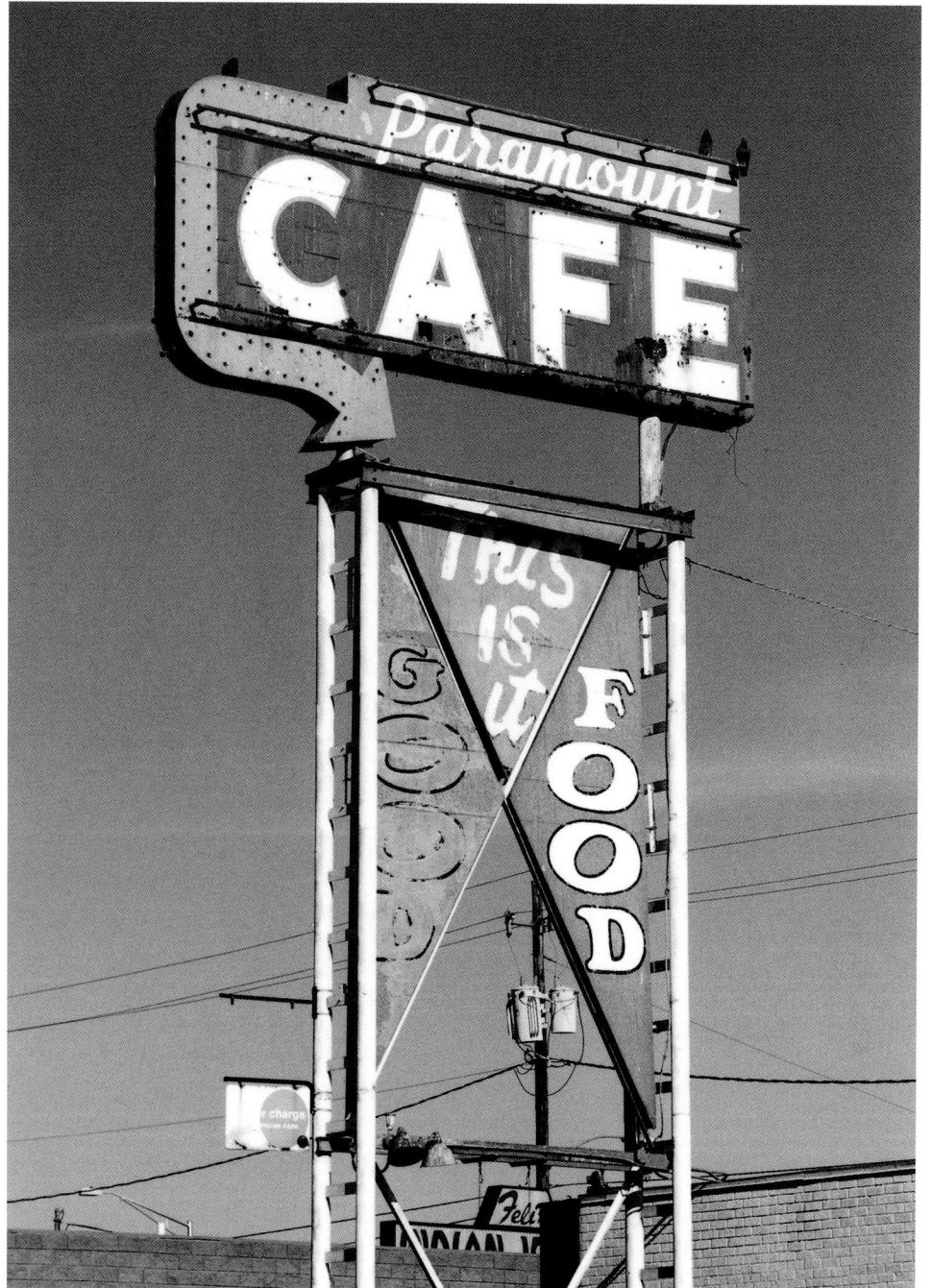

Gallup

N35° 31.5
W108° 45.1

Albuquerque

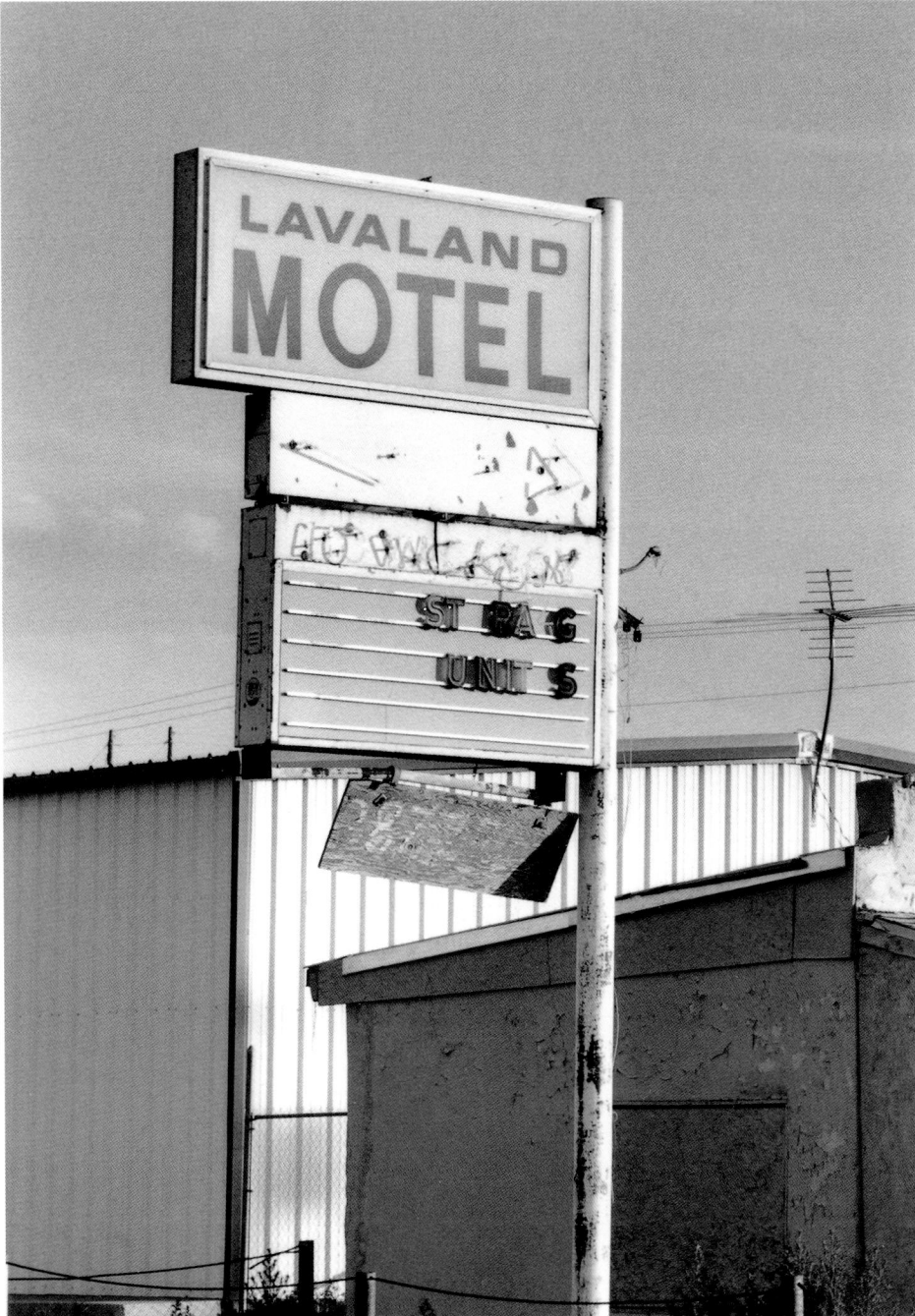

N35° 08.9
W107° 50.7

Grants

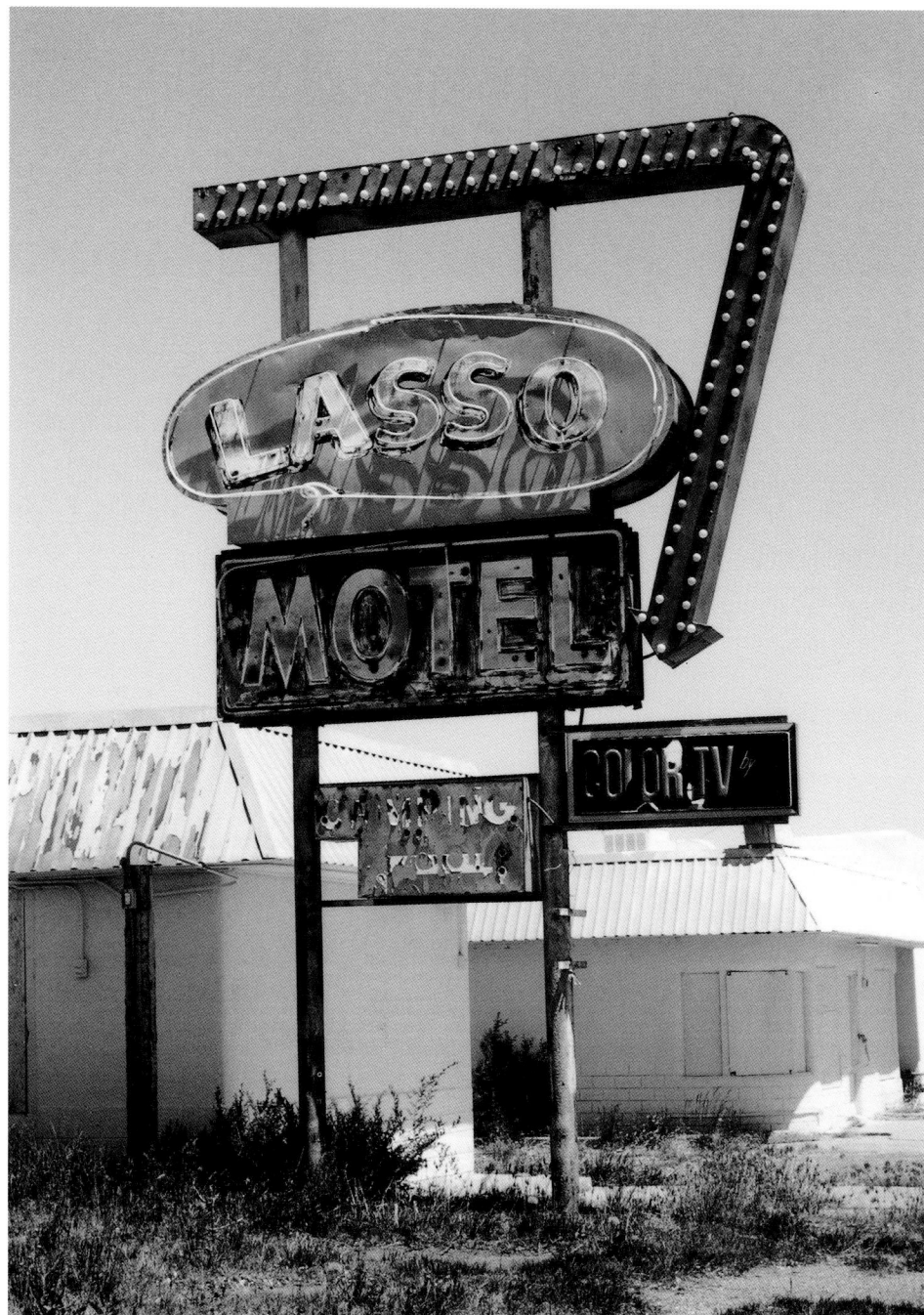

Tucumcari

N35° 10.3
W103° 44.3

N35° 10.3
W103° 44.3

Tucumcari

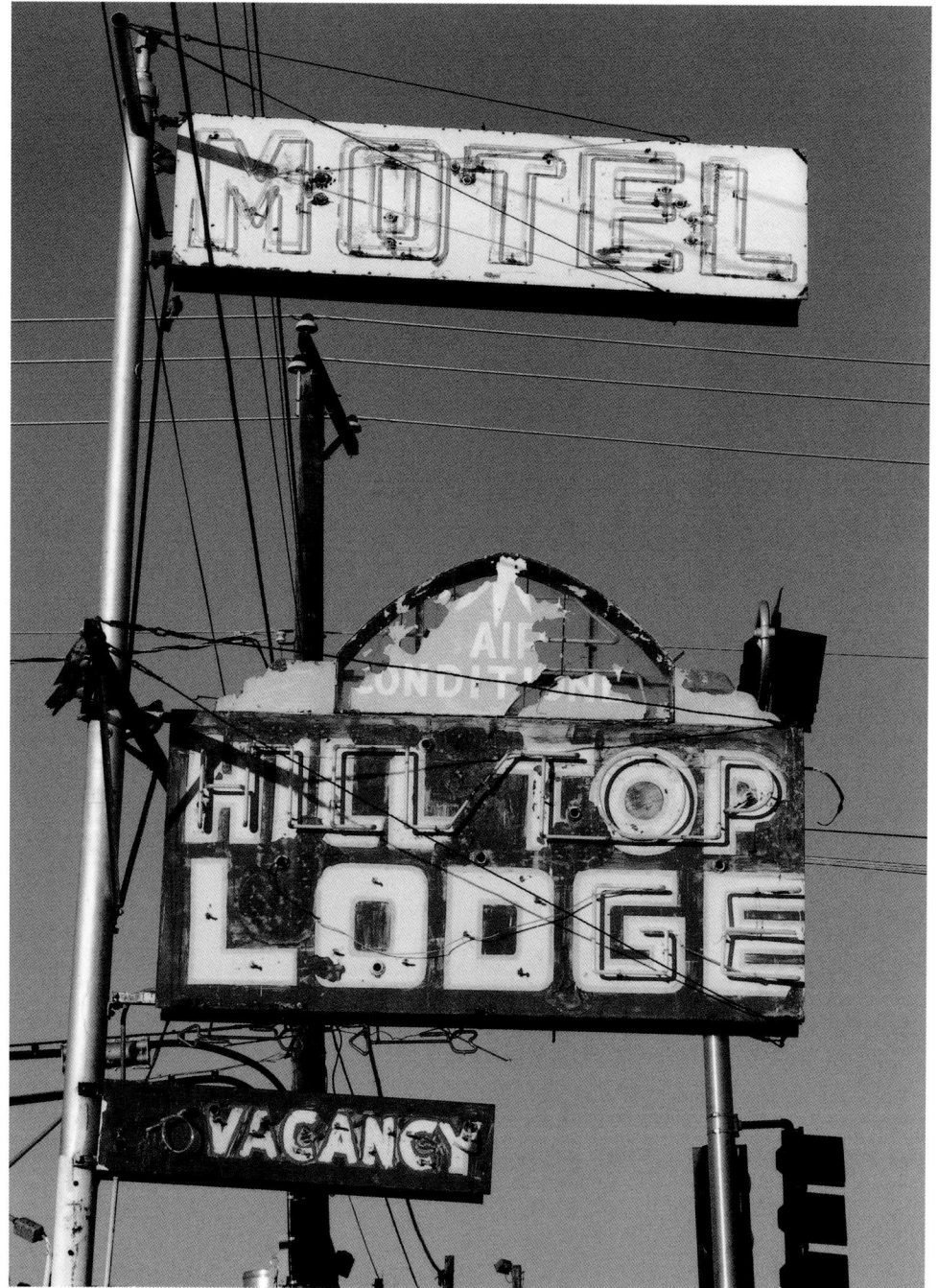

Albuquerque

N35° 05.0
W106° 41.9

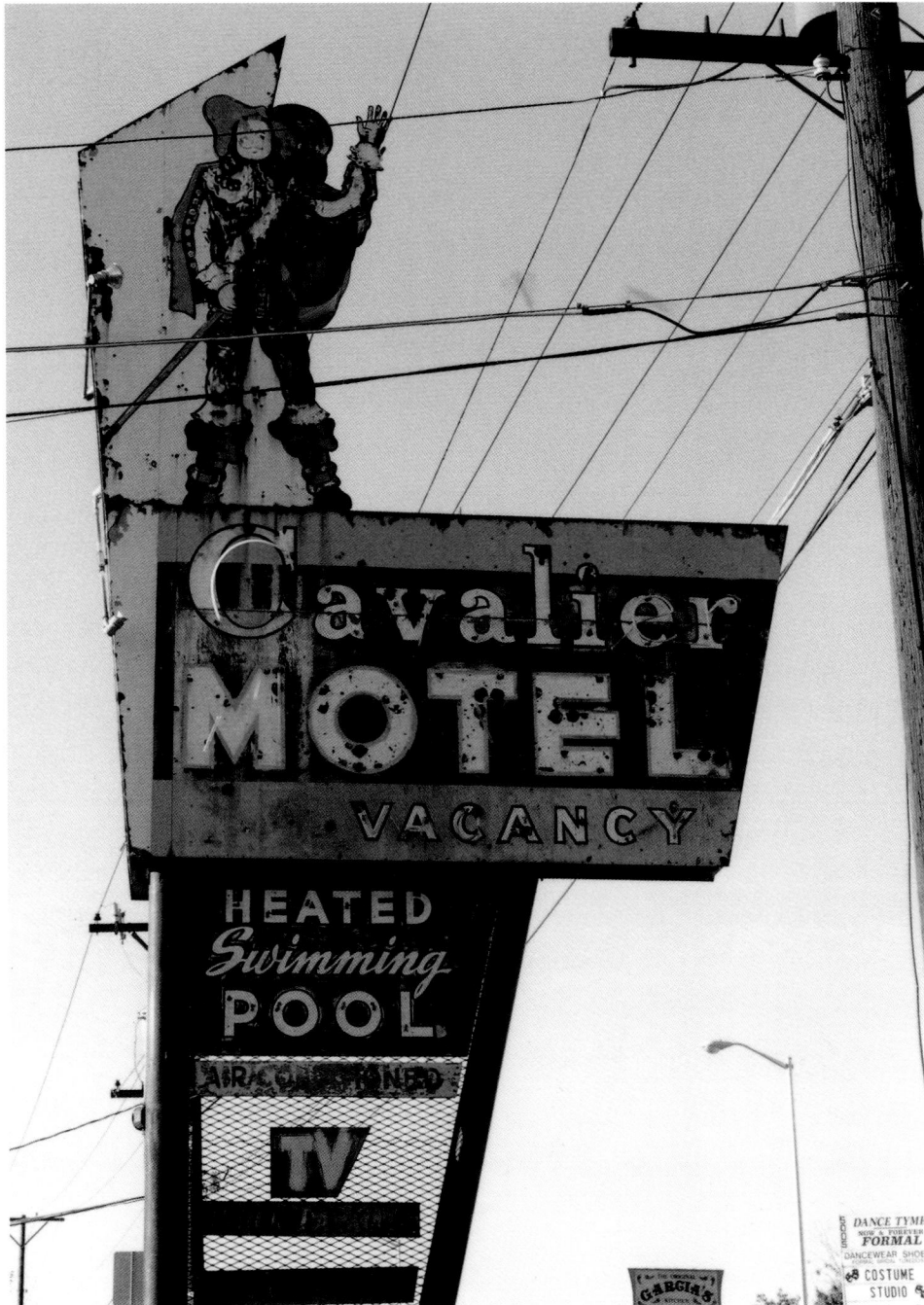

N35° 08.0
W106° 38.5

Albuquerque

Albuquerque

N35° 07.9
W106° 38.5

N35° 25.6
W108° 19.1

Continental Divide

Gallup

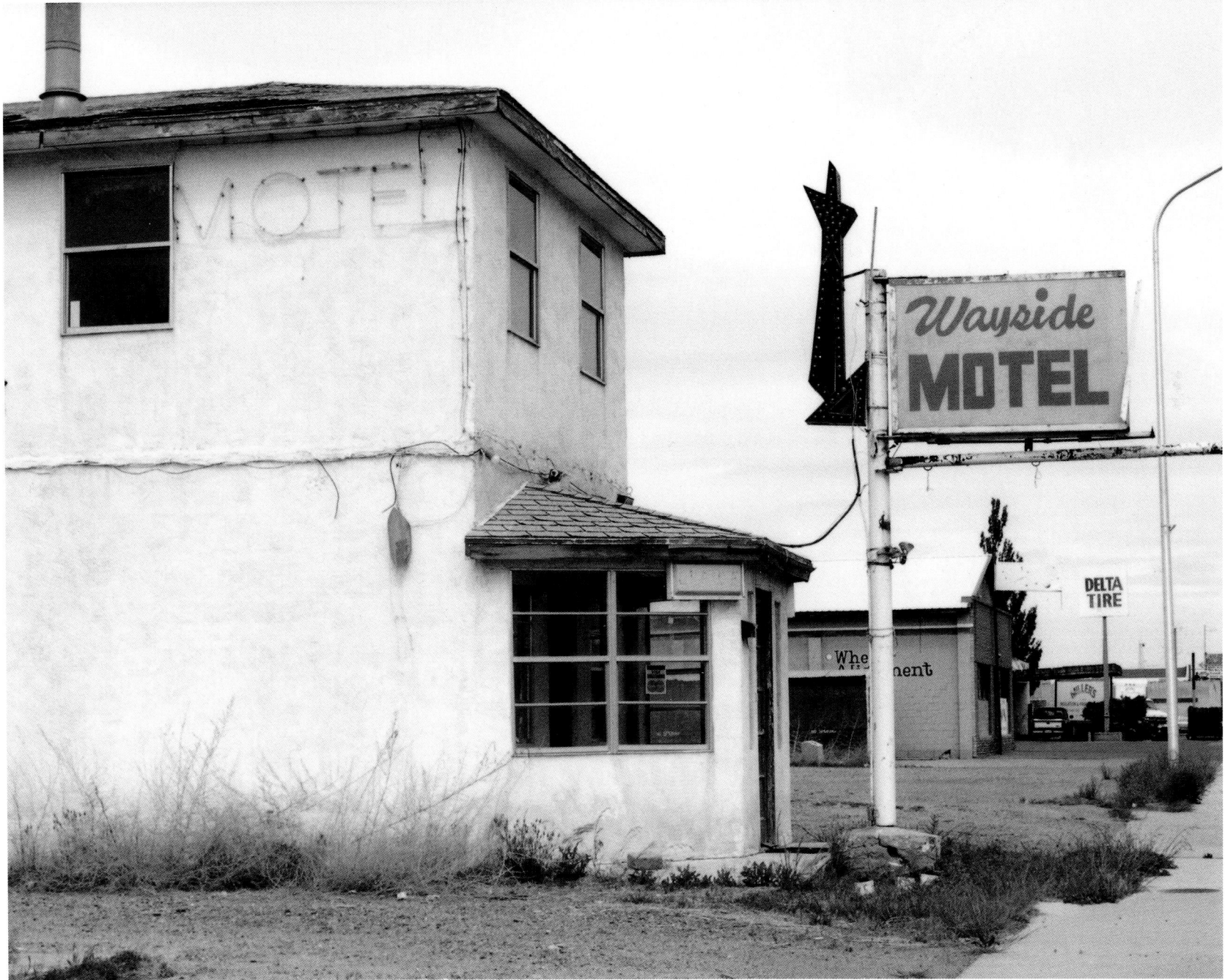

N35° 08.7
W107° 50.4

Grants

Gallup

N35° 31.8
W108° 43.9

N35° 25.6
W108° 19.1

Continental Divide

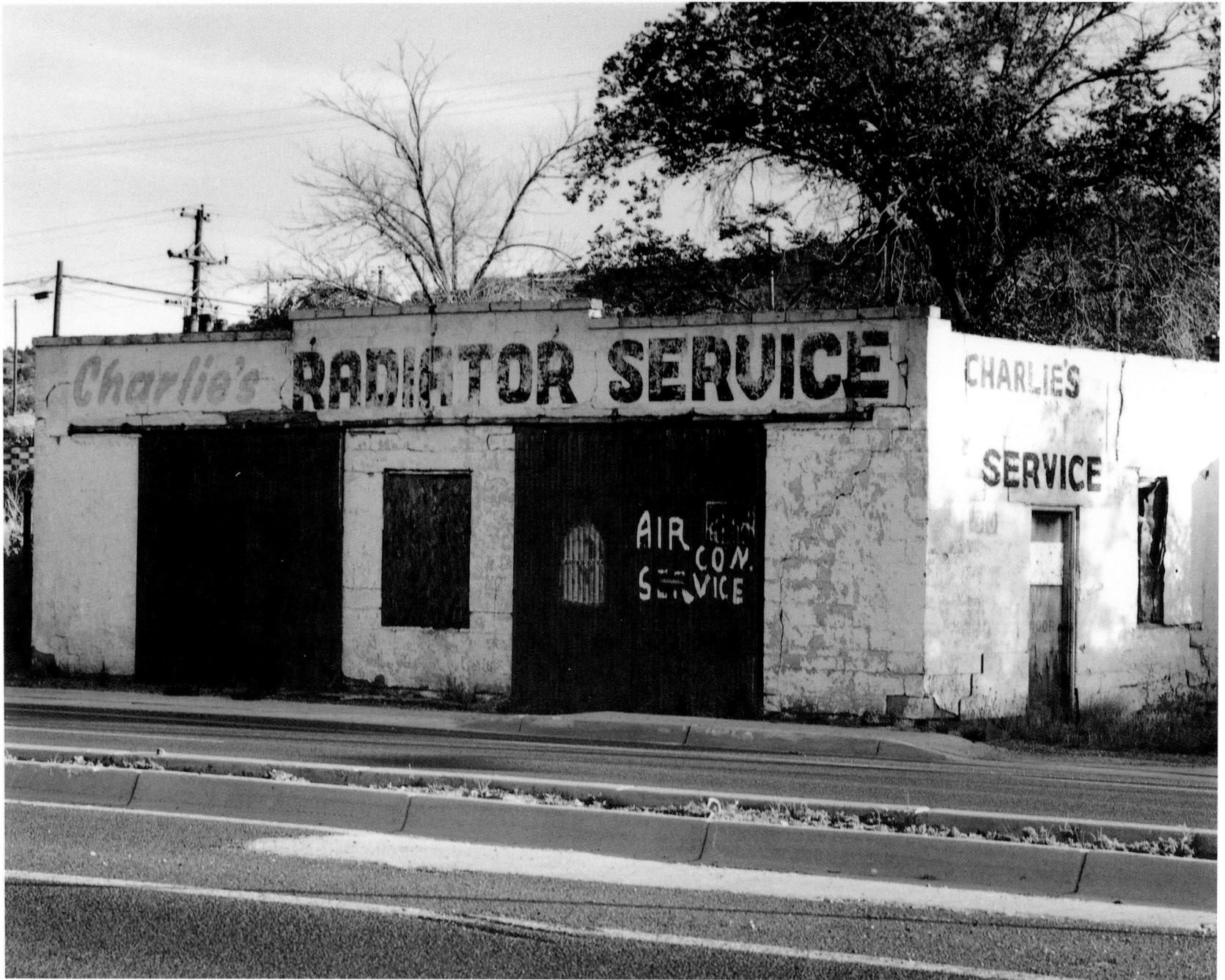

Grants

N35° 09.3
W107° 51.8

The South Side of I-40

N32° 20.7
W108° 41.4

Lordsburg, off I-10

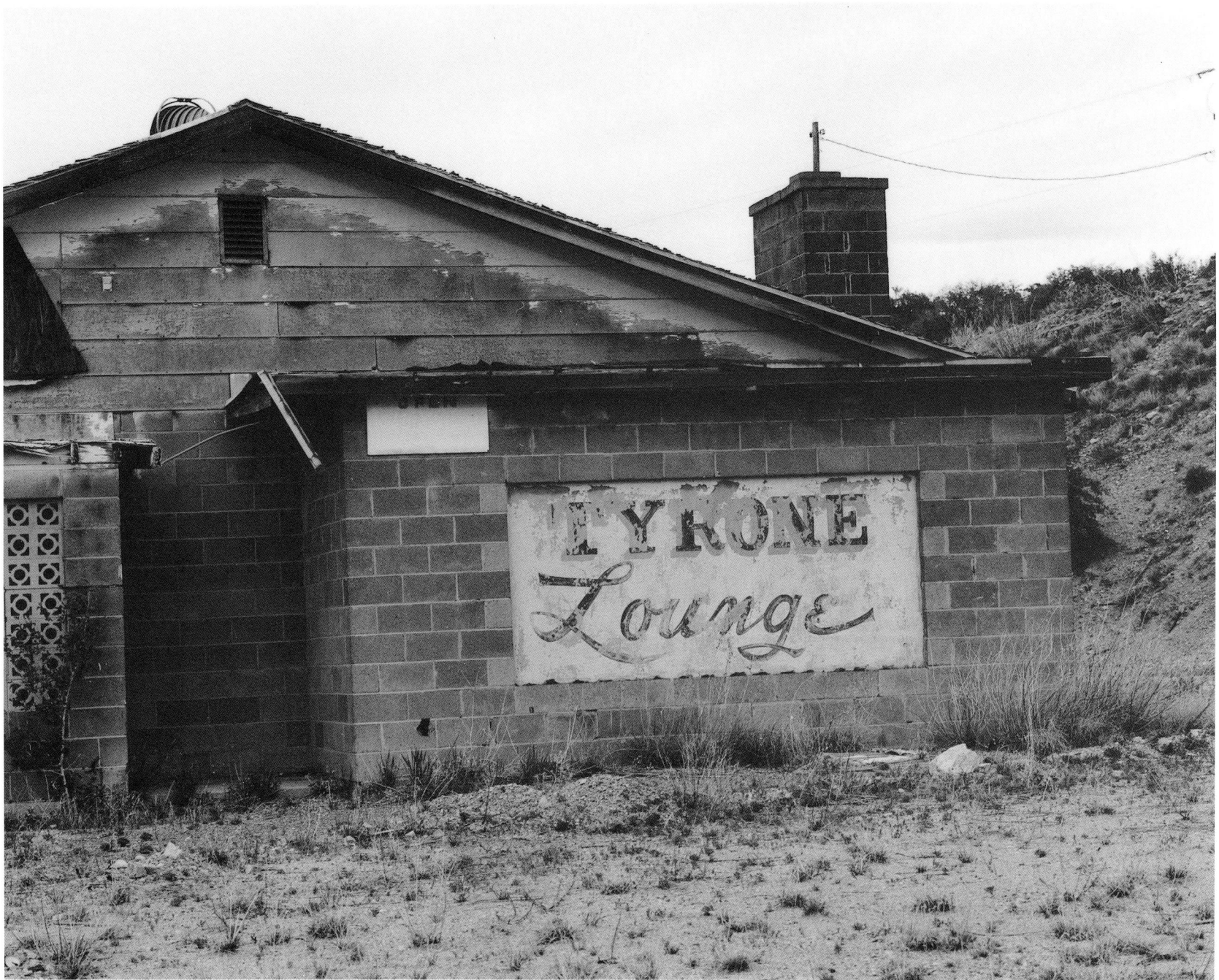

Tyrone, Hwy 90

N32° 40.7
W108° 19.8

N32° 56.9
W105° 57.6

Allamagordo, Hwy 82

Clovis, downtown

N34° 24.0
W103° 12.3

N34° 24.0
W103° 12.2

Clovis, downtown

Silver City, downtown

N32° 46.2
W108° 16.7

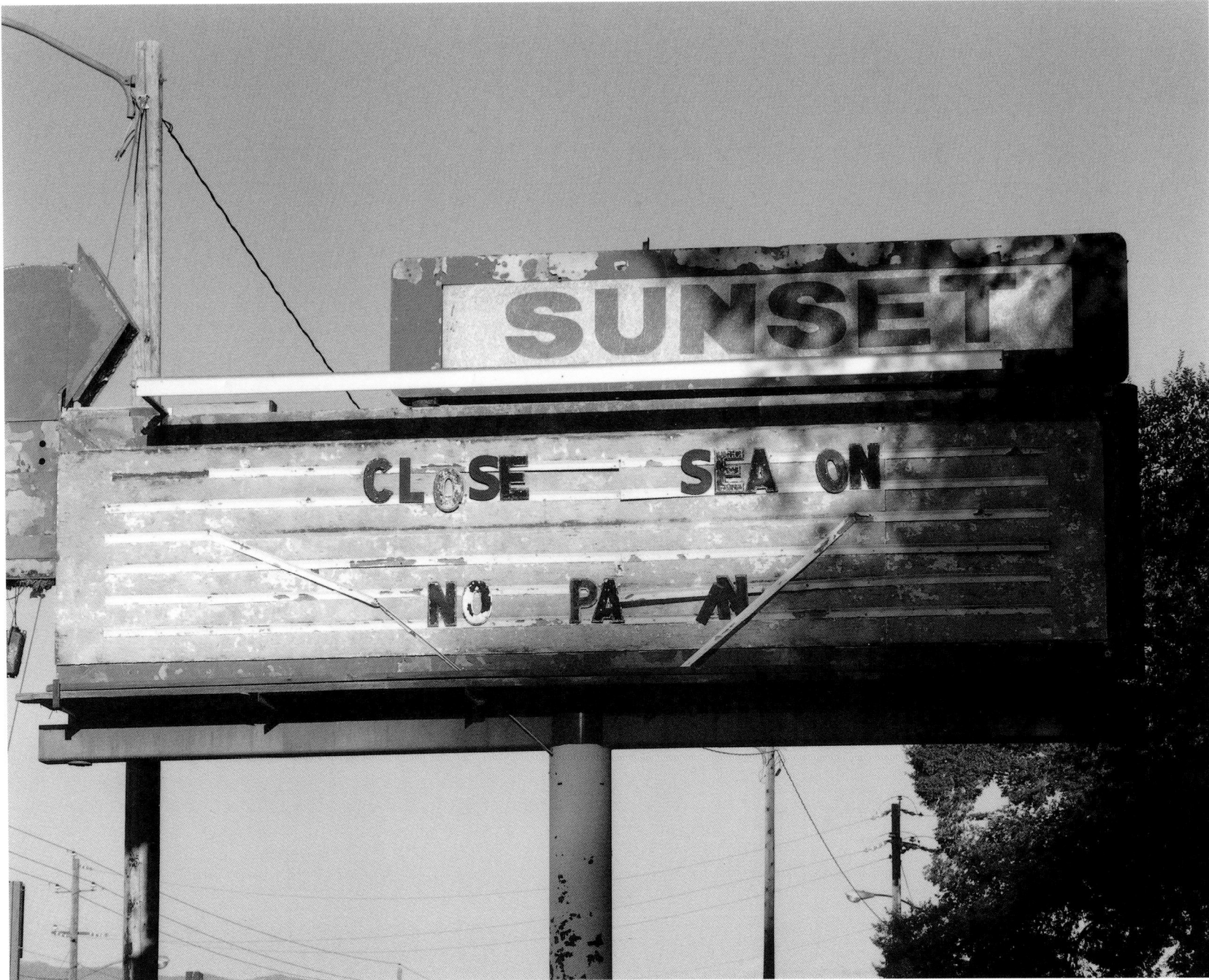

SUNSET

CLOSE SEA ON

NO PA N

N35° 03.2
W106° 40.8

Albuquerque, Arenal Rd.

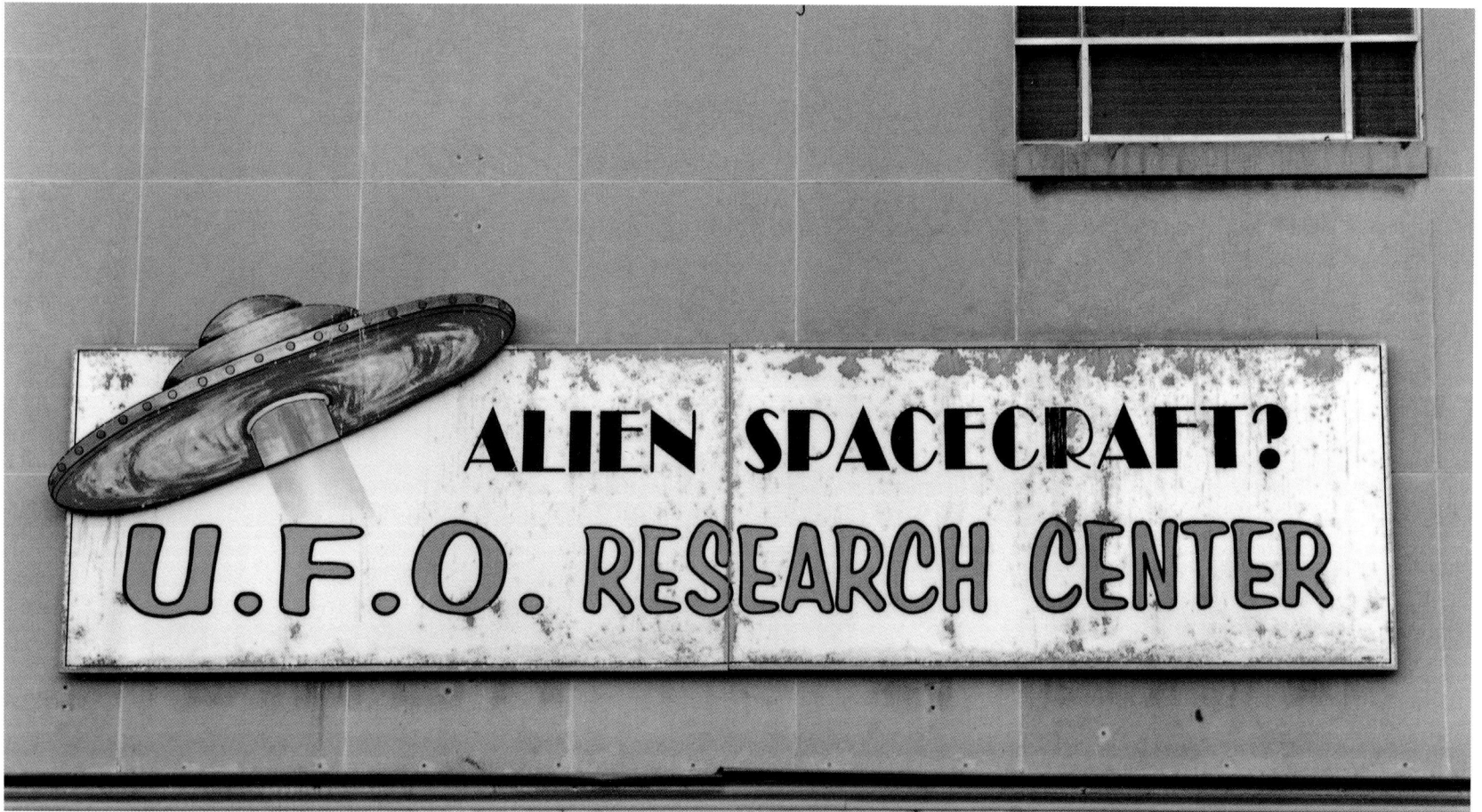

Roswell, downtown

N33° 23.3
W104° 31.4

ALIENS WELCOME

Drive-Thru Service

N33° 24.2
W104° 31.3

Roswell, Hwy 70

Dayton, Hwy 285

N32° 43.7
W104° 23.7

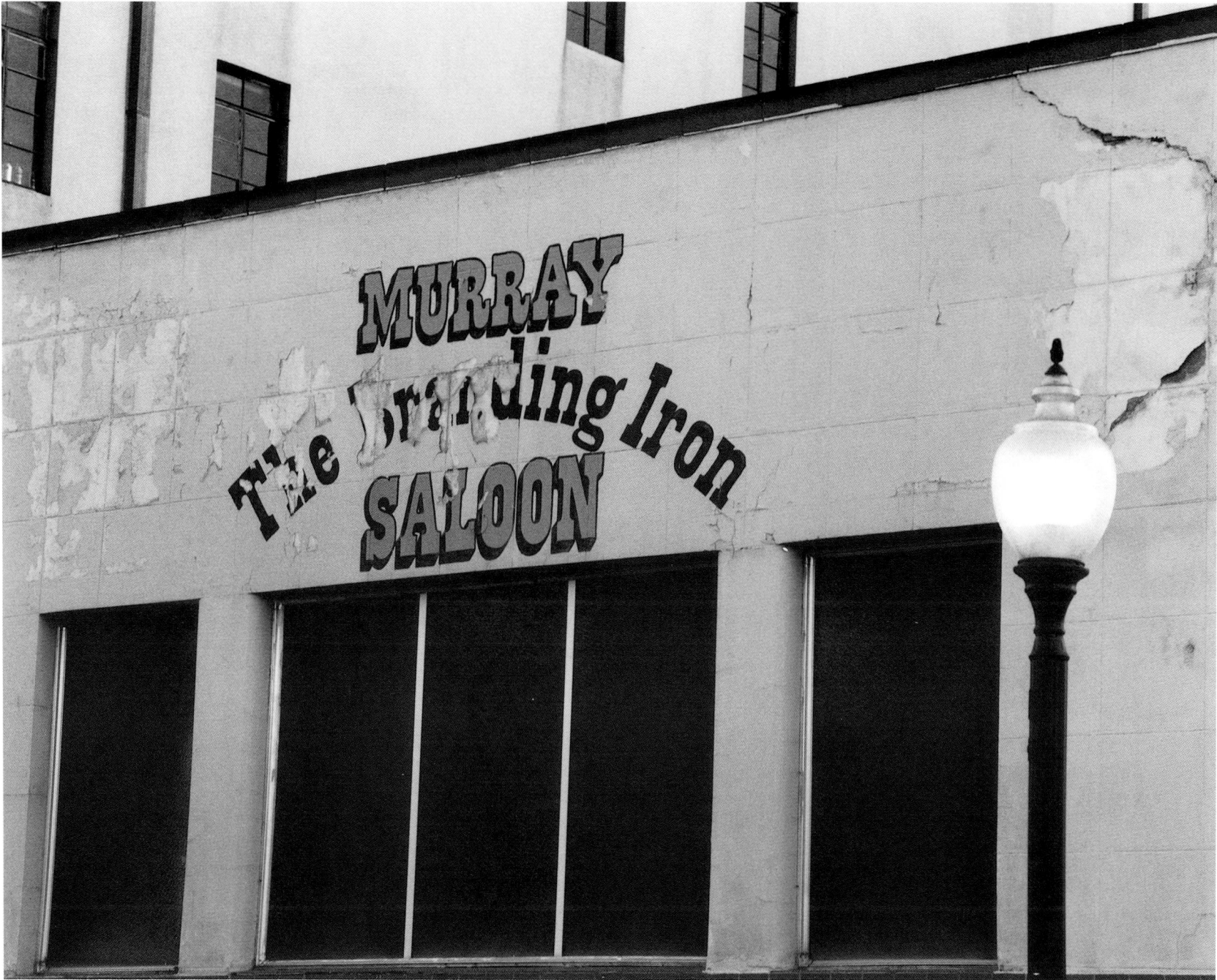

N32° 46.2
W108° 16.7

Silver City, downtown

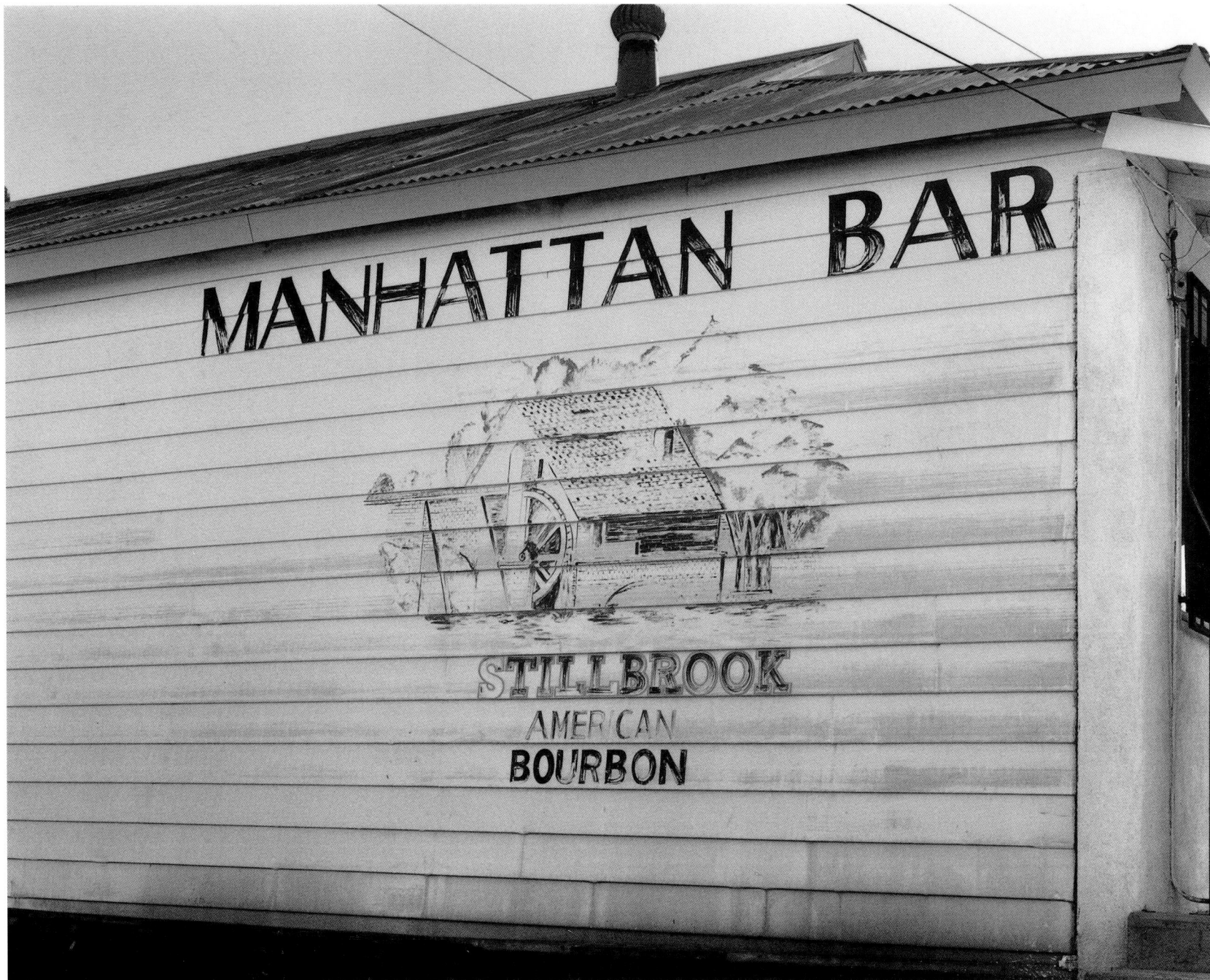

Hanover, Hwy 152

N32° 48.6
W108° 05.4

Socorro, downtown

Hillsboro, Hwy 152

N32° 55.0
W107° 35.1

N34° 56.5
W104° 41.3

west of Santa Rosa, I-40

Pinos Altos, Hwy 15

N32° 52.0
W108° 13.3

Pinos Altos, Hwy 15

Elida, Hwy 70

N33° 56.9
W103° 39.3

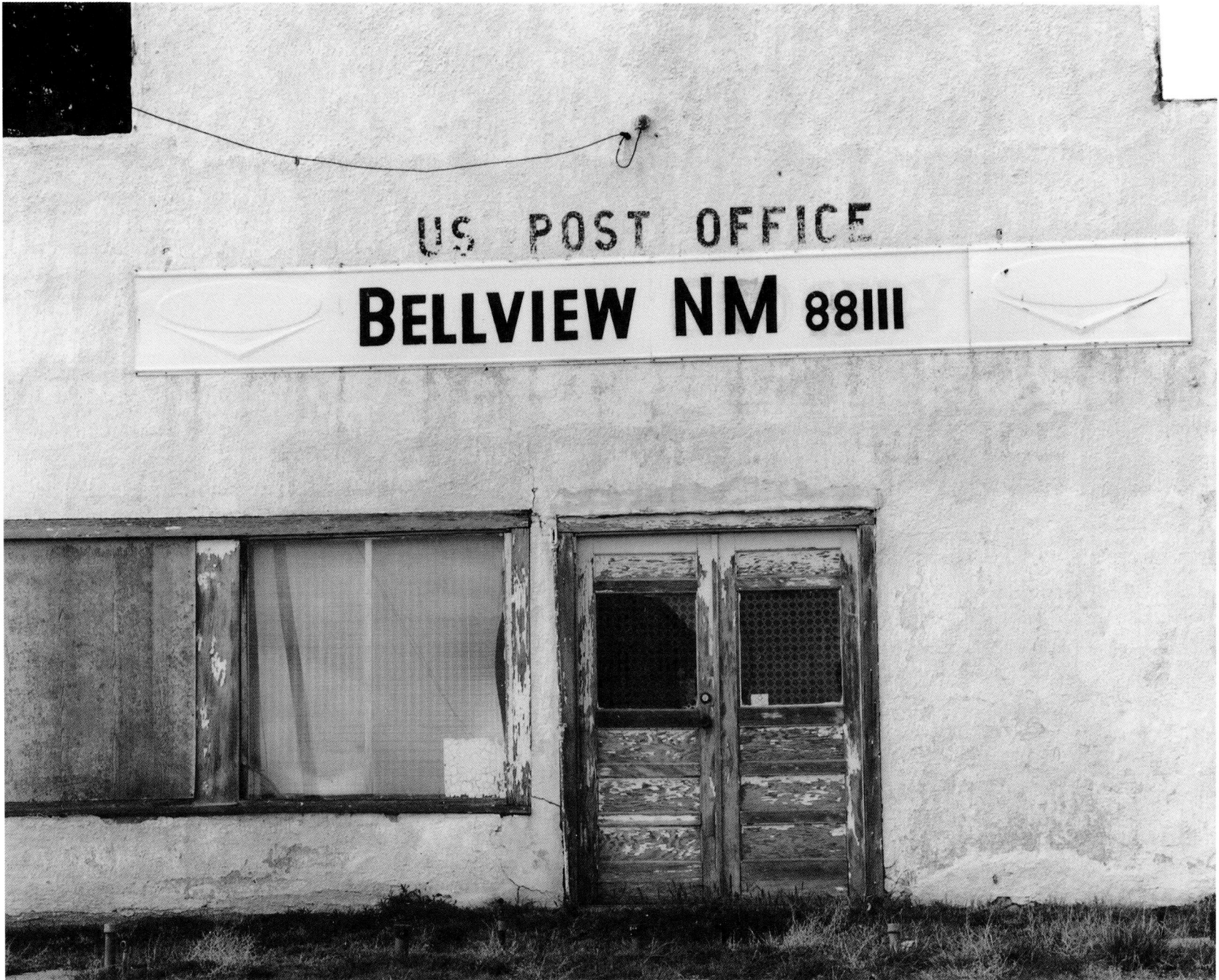

US POST OFFICE

BELLVIEW NM 88111

N34° 49.3
W103° 06.5

Bellview, Hwy 209

San Jon, Hwy 469

N35° 06.4
W103° 19.9

Gallup, downtown

Pinos Altos, Hwy 15

N32° 52.0
W108° 13.3

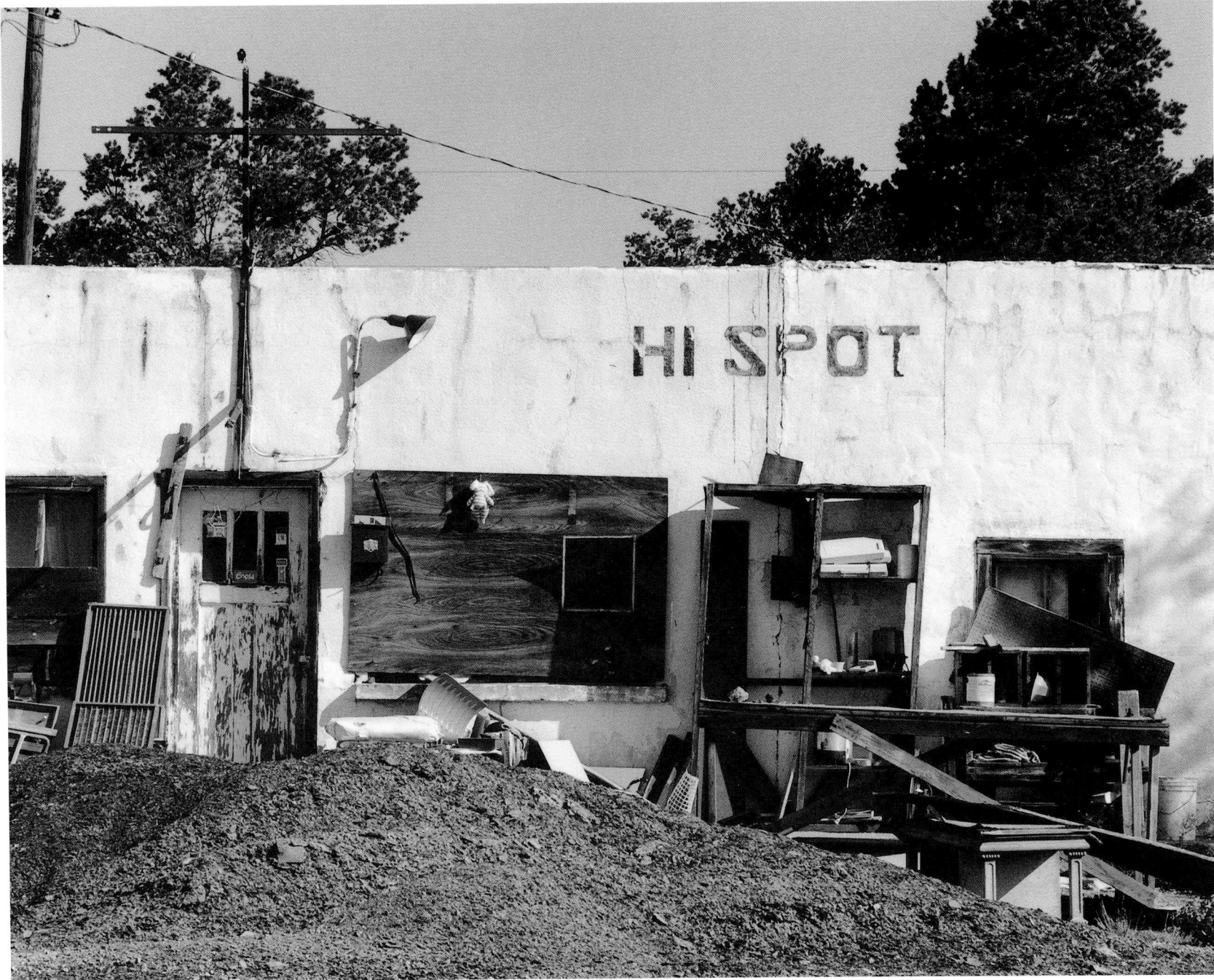

N32° 48.6
W108° 02.0

near Hanover, Hwy 152

Las Cruces, south of I-10

N32° 16.4
W106° 46.0

Zuni, Hwy 53

N35° 04.1
W108° 51.1

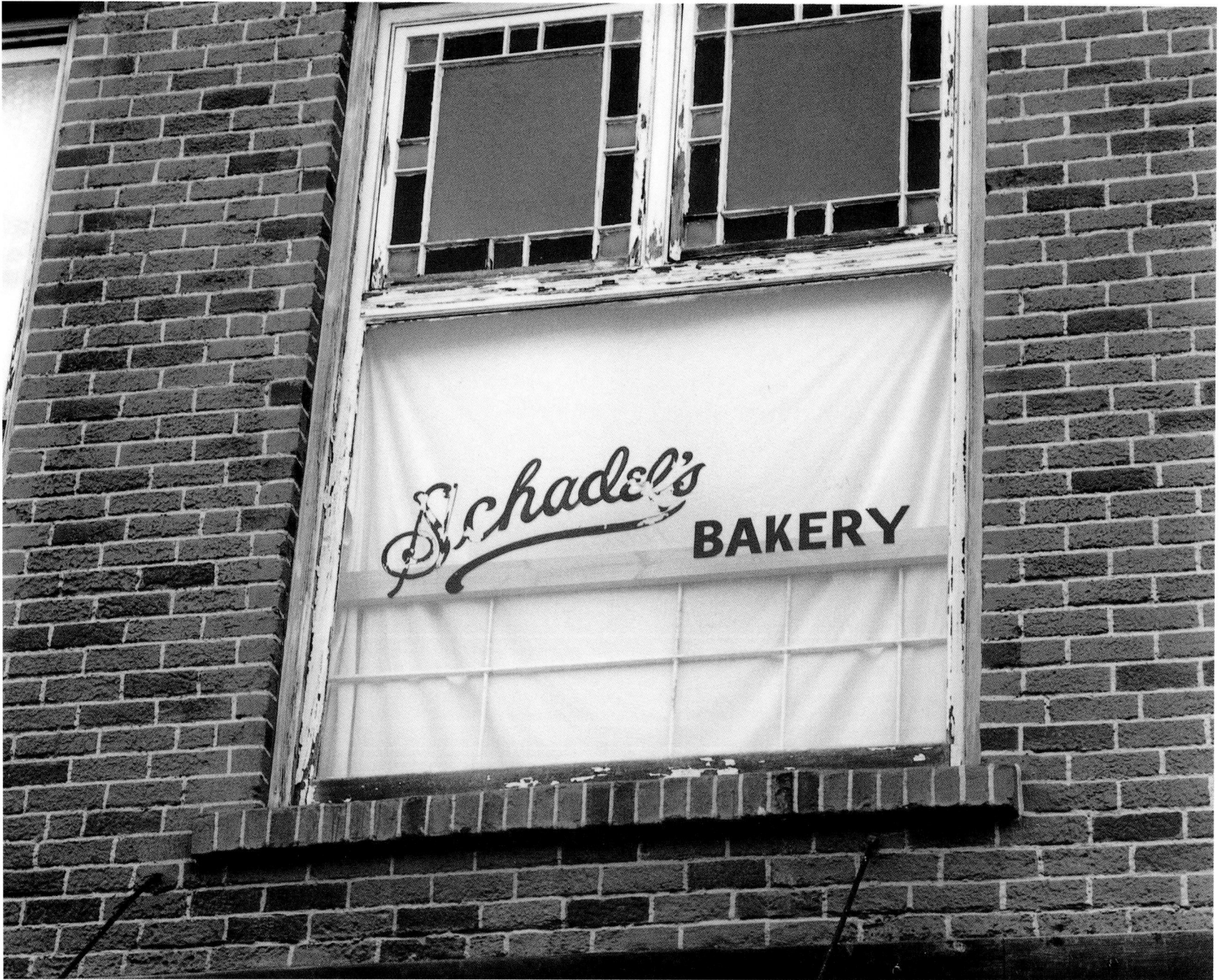

N32° 46.2
W108° 16.7

Silver City, downtown

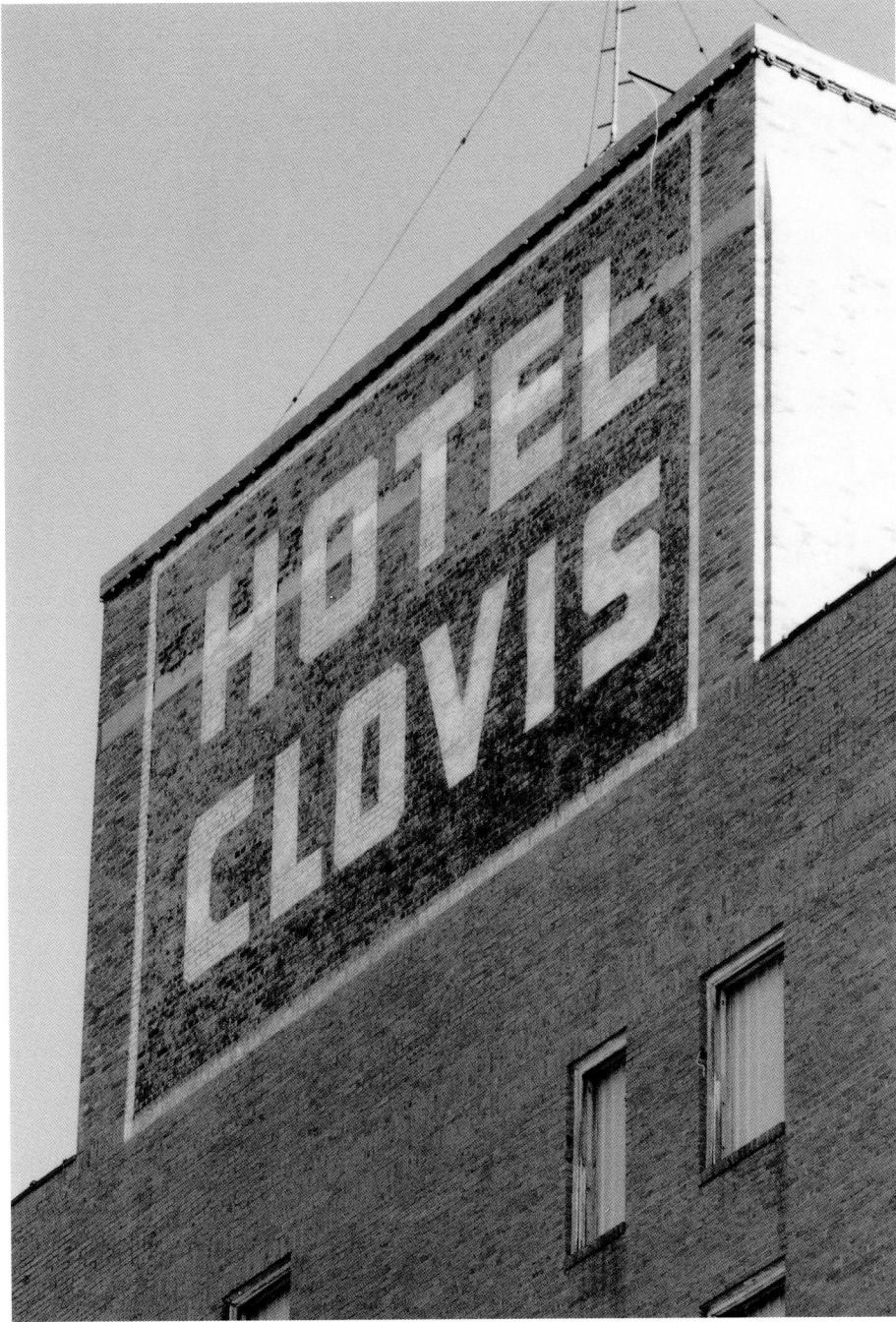

Clovis, downtown

N34° 24.0
W103° 12.3

EST. 1890

Frommer's
TRAVEL GUIDES
1998-1999

N32° 46.2
W108° 16.7

Silver City, downtown

Clovis, downtown

N34° 24.0
W103° 12.3

Silver City, downtown

Socorro, Hwy 60

N34° 03.4
W106° 53.5

N35° 02.4
W108° 58.9

Zuni Pueblo, Hwy 53

May the great ones last.

Silver City, downtown

N32° 24.0
W108° 16.7

N36° 59.5
W106° 30.1

Northern New Mexico/Colorado border, Hwy 17